KT-872-715

Descriptive Cataloging of Rare Materials (Books)

Bibliographic
Standards Committee

Rare Books and
Manuscripts Section

Association of
College and Research
Libraries

IN COLLABORATION WITH

The Cataloging Policy
and Support Office
of the Library of
Congress

Cataloging Distribution Service
Library of Congress
Washington, D.C. 2007

This 2007 publication is a revision of *Descriptive Cataloging of Rare Books*, 1991, itself a revision of *Bibliographic Description of Rare Books*, 1981.

Copyright ©2007 by the Library of Congress except within the U.S.A.

For sale by the Library of Congress Cataloging Distribution Service, 101 Independence Avenue, S.E., Washington, D.C. 20541-4912. Product catalog available on the Web at <http://www.loc.gov/cds>.

ISBN: 978-0-8444-1162-0

LEEDS METROPOLITAN
UNIVERSITY
LIBRARY
1704942998
SuP-B
BP-85668/2009
14.9.07
025.3416 DES

This book is printed on acid-free paper.

Library of Congress Cataloging-in-Publication Data

Association of College and Research Libraries. Rare Books and Manuscripts Section. Bibliographic
    Standards Committee.
    Descriptive cataloging of rare materials (books) / Bibliographic Standards Committee, Rare Books and Manuscripts Section, Association of College and Research Libraries, in collaboration with the Cataloging Policy and Support Office of the Library of Congress.
        p.   cm.

"This 2007 publication is a revision of Descriptive cataloging of rare books, 1991, itself a revision of Bibliographic description of rare books, 1981"--T.p. verso.

Includes bibliographical references and index.

ISBN: 978-0-8444-1162-0 (alk. paper)

1. Cataloging of rare books--Handbooks, manuals, etc. 2. Descriptive cataloging--United States--Handbooks, manuals, etc. 3. Anglo-American cataloguing rules. I. Library of Congress. Cataloging Policy and Support Office. II. Descriptive cataloging of rare books. III. Title. IV. Title: DCRM(B)

Z695.74 .U54 2007

025.3'416--dc22

                                        2006051905

The front cover image is taken from leaf I of Jacobus de Voragine's *Legenda Aurea*, translated into English by William Caxton and printed by Julian Notary in 1504 (Folger shelfmark STC 24877); the back cover image is taken from the colophon of the *Heidelberger Katechismus*, 1584, printed by Matthias Harnisch (Folger shelfmark 218-098.3q).

DCRM(B)

ᵊ Headingley Library  leeds metropolitan university

ı must return this item before the last date
ʙelow.

Leeds Metropolitan University

17 0494299 8

Contents

PREFACE

Background

Descriptive Cataloging of Rare Materials (Books), referred to hereafter as DCRM(B), is third in direct descent from *Bibliographic Description of Rare Books* (BDRB). BDRB was published in 1981 as the interpretations of the Library of Congress for AACR2, rules 2.12-2.18, on early printed monographs. When it was due for revision, the RBMS Bibliographic Standards Committee under Jackie M. Dooley teamed up with Ben R. Tucker and Robert Ewald of the Library of Congress to produce *Descriptive Cataloging of Rare Books* (DCRB), which appeared in 1991. In 1998, Robert L. Maxwell, then chair of the Bibliographic Standards Committee, inaugurated the current revision.

In contrast to the previous two editions of the rare book cataloging rules, the Library of Congress preferred to be responsible for commenting on and approving the text rather than actively engaged in writing it. Director for Cataloging Beacher Wiggins (now Director for Acquisitions and Bibliographic Access) first authorized the revision and the Bibliographic Standards Committee's lead role in it, and Barbara B. Tillett, Chief of the Cataloging Policy and Support Office, confirmed his decision. Along with Elizabeth Robinson (team leader for rare book cataloging), Cataloging Policy and Support Office members Margaret Detweiler and Robert Ewald (both now retired) and Judith Kuhagen have scrutinized drafts and monitored DCRM(B)'s progress.

DCRM(B) was already well underway when work on *RDA: Resource Description and Access* (then called AACR3) was announced. The DCRM(B) editors briefly considered, then rejected, postponing further work until after RDA's publication. We agreed it would be unwise to delay, given the progress already made on DCRM(B) and the considerable investment to date of time, labor, and money.

Changes from DCRB

The most significant changes from DCRB are: new introductory sections on "Objectives and Principles" and "Precataloging Decisions;" the explicit incorporation of machine-made books into the rule text and examples; the addition of Area 6; an expanded appendix on early letter forms and symbols (including images of early letters and symbols accompanied by their correct transcriptions); and new appendixes on collection-level cataloging, core-level cataloging, variations requiring the creation of a new bibliographic record, and individual issues of serials.

DCRM(B) gives expanded guidance and prescribes a more rigorous and consistent approach to transcription than did DCRB, and incorporates a sharp distinction between information transcribed from the source and information that has been supplied by the cataloger. Transcribed information is never to be placed within square brackets (unless the letter or character is unclear; see 0G6.2). Conversely, the presence of square brackets in those areas of the description that require transcription (see introductory section III.2.2) immediately and unambiguously identifies text as supplied or interpolated. Another notable change related to more rigorous transcription principles is that roman dates in the source are transcribed as roman rather than arabic numerals.

Other changes include restricting transcription of the statement of responsibility to the chief source of information; the inclusion of dust jackets as a prescribed source of information for areas 2, 4, and 6; a discussion on the transcription of manufacturers in Area 4; the exclusion of copyright dates from the date of publication element; the elimination of special status for engraved title pages in the statement of extent; the dropping of periods after **cm** and **mm** (approved for AACR2 in 2002 but implementation deferred until publication in RDA), and an expanded section on local notes. Area 0 is substantially re-organized, and the language throughout has been made more consistent and explicit.

Acknowledgments

Many people have contributed their time and effort in bringing DCRM(B) to fruition. Members of the Bibliographic Standards Committee since DCRB went into revision in the spring of 1998:

Randal S. Brandt	Deborah J. Leslie	Nina Schneider
Christine Clarke	Megan Lewis	E.C. Schroeder
Ann W. Copeland	M. Winslow Lundy	Sandra Sider
Laurence S. Creider	Juliet McLaren	Stephen Skuce
Emily Epstein	Russell Martin	Eileen L. Smith
David M. Faulds	Robert L. Maxwell	Joe A. Springer
Sarah Schmidt Fisher	Kate Moriarty	James Stephenson
Jain Fletcher	R. Arvid Nelsen	Bruce Tabb
Jane Gillis	Richard Noble	Manon Théroux
Melinda Hayes	Gregory Pass	Alex Thurman
Eileen Heeran	Elizabeth Robinson	Gerald R. Wager†
Ryan Hildebrand	Jennifer O'Brien Roper	Beth M. Whittaker
James Larrabee	Patrick Russell	

The Bibliographic Standards Committee is profoundly grateful to the Beinecke Rare Book and Manuscript Library of Yale University, for their abundant generosity in bringing twenty-five participants to New Haven for the DCRM Working Conference in 2003, and providing food, housing, space, and staff assistance for an enormously productive four-day meeting. It is not an exaggeration to say that DCRM(B) would have been much the poorer and much the slower without the Beinecke's unstinting support. Conference participants were:

John Attig	Barbara M. Jones	Eileen L. Smith
Ann W. Copeland	James Larrabee	Joe A. Springer
Laurence S. Creider	Deborah J. Leslie	Laura Stalker
Jackie M. Dooley	Robert L. Maxwell	Bruce H. Tabb
Sarah Schmidt Fisher	Juliet McLaren	Suzy Taraba
Jain Fletcher	Gregory A. Pass	Manon Théroux
Jane Gillis	Elizabeth Robinson	Beth M. Whittaker
Brian Hillyard	Jennifer O'Brien Roper	
Elizabeth L. Johnson	Stephen Skuce	

Our heartfelt thanks go, too, to the Folger Shakespeare Library for generously providing meeting space for three DCRM(B) editorial meetings. All images come from the collections of the Folger Shakespeare Library.

Conscientious and insightful comment on earlier drafts of DCRM(B) was provided by the Rare Books Department of Cambridge University Library; the Bibliographic Standards Committee of the Rare Books and Special Collections Group, Chartered Institute of Library and Information Professionals (UK); CC:DA; the Rare Book Team of Yale University Library, and of course our partner in this endeavor, the Cataloging Policy and Support Office of the Library of Congress.

We extend our warm gratitude to all those who, in addition to those listed above, contributed to DCRM(B) by participating actively at the public hearing, commenting on or proofreading drafts, and providing valuable research and expert opinion. This is surely a community document: Karen Attar, Dorothy Auyong, Matthew Beacom, Erin C. Blake, Ronald Bogdan, J.P. Brigham, Lyle E. Buettner, Deanna Chavez, Ellen Ellickson, Will Evans, Todd Fell, Carol Fink, Lisa Furubotten, Benjamin Griffin, John J. Hall, Matthew Heintzelman, Barry E. Hinman, Eric Holzenberg, Nancy A. Kandoian, Jim Kuhn, Daniel Lovins, Lucy Marks, Alexandra Mason, Christopher S. Motta, Walter F. Nickeson, Michael North, Doris N. O'Keefe, Carol E. Pardo, Mitchell Pendleton, Sara Piasecki, Daniel Rettberg, Joseph Ripp, Joseph Ross, Lenore M. Rouse, Christopher Smith, Karen Spicher, Stephen Tabor, Penny Welbourne, Kathleen Whalen, Jane Wickenden, David Woodruff, and Stephen R. Young.

The scores of students who have passed through my Rare Book School cataloging course at the University of Virginia, and now, California, have helped shape this document immeasurably, whether they know it or not. By applying their fresh and inquisitive minds to DCRB and the drafts of DCRM(B), they have kept my own from the dangers of a blindness born of too-long acquaintance.

The index was prepared by Jean Skipp of IncludesIndex. The cover and title page design is by Kathy Bowlin of Graphic Answers Inc.

Finally, I want to acknowledge and thank the four people who agreed to serve with me as DCRM(B) editors, who have given generously of their time and considerable intellect; it has been a delight as well as an education working with them: John Attig, Robert L. Maxwell, Joe A. Springer, and Manon Théroux. Editors preparing the other DCRM components have as well provided smart, substantive, cheerful, and most welcome editorial help and advice: Randal S. Brandt, Ann W. Copeland, Jain Fletcher, Jane Gillis, Juliet McLaren, and Stephen Skuce.

Manon Théroux deserves special recognition: as chair of the Editorial Team, she has devoted uncountable hours (many of them while the rest of us slept, not to mention postponing her honeymoon) to organizing the work of the editorial team, setting meeting agendas, keeping track of its progress, taking up the slack when assigned tasks fell through, carefully evaluating each proposed change and addition, writing portions of new text, and making painstaking, well-documented edits. My esteem, gratitude, and admiration know no bounds.

Deborah J. Leslie
Chair, RBMS Bibliographic Standards Committee
7 December 2006

Introduction

Contents:

I. Scope and purpose

I.1. Descriptive Cataloging of Rare Materials

DCRM(B) is the first of several manuals providing specialized cataloging rules for various formats of rare materials typically found in rare book, manuscript, and special collection repositories.[1] Together, these manuals form Descriptive Cataloging of Rare Materials (DCRM), an overarching concept rather than a publication in its own right. DCRM component manuals for serials and music are in preparation. Other components will be added to the DCRM family as they are developed.

I.2. Descriptive Cataloging of Rare Materials (Books)

DCRM(B) provides guidelines and instructions for descriptive cataloging of rare books, that is, printed textual monographs receiving special treatment within a repository. Unlike its predecessors, which were intended to apply exclusively to pre-1801 imprints, DCRM(B) may be used for printed monographs of any age or type of production. Rare maps, music, serials, and manuscripts of any type are

---

[1] The term "rare materials" is used to refer to any special materials that repositories have chosen to distinguish from general materials by the ways in which they house, preserve, or collect them. Rarity in the narrow sense of "scarce" may or may not be a feature of these materials.

out of scope, with the exception of individual and special issues of serials treated as monographs (see Appendix H).

I.3 Need for special rules

Printed materials in special collections often present situations not ordinarily encountered in the cataloging of typical modern publications (e.g., variation between copies, cancelled leaves, etc.) and may require additional details of description in order to identify significant characteristics (e.g., bibliographical format, typeface, etc.). Such details are important for two reasons. They permit the ready identification of copies of a resource (e.g., as editions, impressions, or issues), and they provide a more exact description of the resource as an artifact.

I.4. Scope of application

DCRM(B) is especially appropriate for the description of publications produced before the introduction of machine printing in the nineteenth century. However, it may be used to describe any printed monograph, including machine-press publications, artists' books, private press books, and other contemporary materials.

These rules may be applied categorically to books based on date or place of publication (e.g., all British and North American imprints published before 1831), or may be applied selectively, according to the administrative policy of the institution, which may choose to catalog some or all of its holdings at a more detailed level of description than that provided for in AACR2. (See introductory section X.1 for discussion on choosing appropriate cataloging codes and levels.)

I.5. Application within the bibliographic record

These rules contain instructions for the descriptive elements in bibliographic records only. They do not address the construction and assignment of controlled headings used as main and added entries, although brief instructions relating to headings and other access points do appear throughout (e.g., Appendix F is entirely devoted to recommendations for uncontrolled title added entries).

II. Relationship to other standards

II.1. AACR2, ISBD(A), and other cataloging documentation

As a revision of DCRB, DCRM(B) is based on AACR2 as amended by the *Library of Congress Rule Interpretations* (LCRI), as well as on the second edition of ISBD(A). The Library of Congress authorizes DCRM(B) as its interpretation of AACR2, 2.12-18. DCRM(B) deviates in substance from AACR2 and LCRI only when required by the particular descriptive needs of rare materials. In matters of style, presentation, wording, and subarrangement within areas, DCRM(B) follows its own conventions.

Refer to AACR2 and LCRI for guidance and instructions on matters of description not covered in DCRM(B). The relevant sections of AACR2 and LCRI must be consulted for rules governing name and uniform title headings to be used as access points for authors, editors, illustrators, printers, series, etc. For subject headings, numerous controlled vocabularies are available; within the United States, the subject headings of the Library of Congress are widely used. Consult classification documentation for assignment of call numbers. For genre/form headings, consult the various specialized thesauri issued by the RBMS Bibliographic Standards Committee.[2] Terms from other authorized thesauri (e.g., the *Art and Architecture Thesaurus*) may also be used as appropriate.

II.2. MARC 21

MARC 21 Format for Bibliographic Data is the presumed format for presentation and communication of machine-readable cataloging. Use of DCRM(B), however, need not be restricted to a machine environment, and MARC 21 is not mandatory. Examples in the body of DCRM(B) are shown using ISBD punctuation; use of MARC 21 coding appears only in some of the appendixes. Catalogers using MARC 21 should follow MARC 21 documentation for input, and be aware of how their bibliographic systems interpret MARC 21 codes to automatically generate display features. This usually means, for example, that the cataloger omits punctuation between areas, parentheses enclosing a series statement, and certain words prefacing formal notes.

---

[2] These thesauri include: *Binding Terms*; *Genre Terms*; *Paper Terms*; *Printing and Publishing Evidence*; *Provenance Evidence*; and *Type Evidence*.

III. Objectives and principles

The instructions contained in DCRM are formulated according to the objectives and principles set forth below. These objectives and principles seek to articulate the purpose and nature of specialized cataloging rules for rare materials. They are informed by long-accepted concepts in bibliographic scholarship and the Anglo-American cataloging tradition, as well as by more recent theoretical work important to the construction and revision of cataloging codes, namely the International Federation of Library Associations and Institutions' *Functional Requirements for Bibliographic Records* (FRBR) and Elaine Svenonius's *The Intellectual Foundation of Information Organization*. They assume familiarity with the FRBR terms used to categorize entities that are the products of intellectual or artistic endeavor (work, expression, manifestation, and item) as well as bibliographic terms used to differentiate among textual variants (edition, issue, impression, and state). It is hoped that these objectives and principles will provide catalogers, and administrators of cataloging operations, with a better understanding of the underlying rationale for DCRM instructions.

III.1. Functional objectives of DCRM

The primary objectives in cataloging rare materials are no different from those in cataloging other materials. These objectives focus on meeting user needs to find, identify, select, and obtain materials. However, users of rare materials often bring specialized requirements to these tasks that cannot be met by general cataloging rules, such as those contained in the latest revision of AACR2. In addition, the standard production practices assumed in general cataloging rules do not always apply to rare materials. The following DCRM objectives are designed to accommodate these important differences.

III.1.1. Users must be able to distinguish clearly among different manifestations of an expression of a work

The ability to distinguish among different manifestations of an expression of a work is critical to the user tasks of identifying and selecting bibliographic resources. In general cataloging codes like AACR2, it is assumed that abbreviated and normalized transcription is sufficient to distinguish among manifestations. Users of rare materials, however, often require fuller, more faithful transcriptions, greater detail in the physical description area, and careful recording of various distinguishing points in the note area, in order to identify separate manifestations. Additionally, users of rare materials are typically interested in drawing finer distinctions among variants within manifestations than are users of other materials, including not simply between editions and issues but between variant impressions and states; many also need to distinguish between copies at the item level.

III.1.2. Users must be able to perform most identification and selection tasks without direct access to the materials

Users of rare materials frequently perform identification and selection tasks under circumstances that require the bibliographic description to stand as a detailed surrogate for the item (e.g., consultation from a distance, limited access due to the fragile condition of the item, inability to physically browse collections housed in restricted areas, etc.). Accuracy of bibliographic representation increases subsequent efficiency for both users and collection managers. The same accuracy contributes to the long-term preservation of the materials themselves, by reducing unnecessary circulation and examination of materials that do not precisely meet users' requirements.

III.1.3. Users must be able to investigate physical processes and post-production history and context exemplified in materials described

Users of rare materials routinely investigate a variety of artifactual and post-production aspects of materials. For example, they may want to locate materials that are related by printing methods, illustration processes, binding styles and structures, provenance, genre/form, etc. The ability of users to identify materials that fit these criteria depends upon full and accurate descriptions and the provision of appropriate access points.

III.1.4. Users must be able to gain access to materials whose production or presentation characteristics differ from modern conventions

In order to distinguish among manifestations, general cataloging codes like AACR2 rely on explicit bibliographic evidence presented in conventional form (e.g., a formal edition statement on the title page or its verso). In rare materials, such explicit evidence will often be lacking or insufficient to distinguish among different manifestations. That which is bibliographically significant may thus be obscured.

III.2. Principles of DCRM construction

To meet the objectives listed above, DCRM relies upon the following six principles. These principles are influenced by the general principles of bibliographic description offered by Svenonius: user convenience; representation; sufficiency and necessity; standardization; and integration.

III.2.1. Rules provide guidance for descriptions that allow users to distinguish clearly among different manifestations of an expression of a work

This principle derives from the general principle of user convenience and has implications for all areas of the bibliographic description. The principle relates to objective 1 stated above.

III.2.2. Rules provide for accurate representations of the entity as it describes itself, notably through instructions regarding transcription, transposition, and omission

This principle derives from the general principles of representation (with its related subprinciple of accuracy) and of standardization. Precise representation is of particular relevance in those areas of the description that require transcription (the title and statement of responsibility area, the edition area, the publication, distribution, etc., area, and the series area), but should not be ignored in the physical description and note areas. The general principles of representation and standardization stand in greater tension with each other when cataloging rare materials. Faithfulness to both principles may require descriptive and annotative treatment necessarily exceeding the norms (and at times the vocabulary) established as sufficient for the description of general materials. The principle relates to objectives 2 and 4 stated above.

III.2.3. Rules provide guidance for the inclusion of manifestation-specific and item-specific information that permits users to investigate physical processes and post-production history and context exemplified in the item described

This principle derives from the general principle of sufficiency and necessity (with its related subprinciple of significance). Application of the principle requires that rules for rare materials cataloging provide additional guidance on access points, particularly in cases where such information is not integral to the manifestation, expression, or work described. Rules for item-specific information appearing in the note area may recommend standard forms for presentation of information (addressing the general principle of user convenience and its related subprinciple of common usage). Application of such rules presumes both a user's need for such information and a cataloger's ability to properly describe such aspects. The principle relates to objective 3 stated above.

III.2.4. Rules provide for the inclusion of all elements of bibliographical significance

General cataloging codes like AACR2 routinely strive for both brevity and clarity, principles affiliated with the general principle of sufficiency. In describing rare materials, too great an emphasis on brevity may become the occasion for insufficiency and lack of clarity. Brevity of description may be measured best against the functional requirements of the particular bibliographic description rather than against the average physical length of other bibliographic descriptions in the catalog. The tension between rules for rare materials that promote accurate representation of an item and yet do not exceed the requirements of sufficiency is great. Reference to the principle of user convenience may offer correct resolution of such tensions. This principle is related to all of the objectives stated above.

III.2.5. Rules conform to the substance and structure of the latest revision of AACR2 to the extent possible; ISBD(A) serves as a secondary reference point

This principle relates to general principles of standardization and user convenience (with the latter's subprinciple of common usage). DCRM assumes that users of bibliographic descriptions constructed in accordance with its provisions operate in contexts where AACR2 (often as interpreted and applied by the Library of Congress) is the accepted standard for the cataloging of general materials. Therefore, DCRM uses existing AACR2 vocabulary in a manner consistent with AACR2; any additional specialized vocabulary necessary for description and access of rare materials occurs in a clear and consistent manner in DCRM rules, appendixes, and glossary entries. DCRM does not introduce rules that are not required by differences expected between rare and general materials. Numbering of areas within DCRM conforms to the structure of ISBD as implemented in AACR2. When an existing AACR2 rule satisfies the requirements of cataloging rare materials, DCRM text is modeled on AACR2 text (substituting examples drawn from rare materials for illustration). In cases where the language of AACR2 is not precise enough to convey necessary distinctions or may introduce confusion when dealing with rare materials, DCRM uses carefully considered alternative wording. Wording of relevant ISBD(A) standards was also considered when deviating from AACR2.

III.2.6. Rules are compatible with DCRB except in cases where changes are necessary to align more closely to current revisions of AACR2 or to conform to the above principles

This principle relates to general principles of standardization and user convenience (with the latter's subprinciple of common usage). DCRM assumes that users of bibliographic descriptions constructed in accordance with its provisions operate in contexts where monographic materials in special collections were cataloged, until recently, using DCRB. Therefore, changes to DCRB cataloging practices were introduced only after careful consideration of the value or necessity of such changes.

IV. Options

Available options are indicated in one of three ways.

- ‣ Alternative rule designates an alternative option which affects all or several areas of the description, and which must be used consistently throughout. In DCRM(B), alternative rules apply to the transcription of original punctuation and to the creation of separate records for individual impressions, states, binding variants, or copies.

- ‣ *"Optionally"* introduces an alternative treatment of an element.

- ‣ "If considered important" indicates that more information may be added in a note, and thus signals choices for more or less depth in the description. This phrase covers the entire range between best practice on the one end, and highly specialized practices on the other.

The cataloging agency may wish to establish policies and guidelines on the application of options, leave the use of options to the discretion of the cataloger, or use a combination of the two.

V. Language preferences

DCRM(B) is written for an English-speaking context. Cataloging agencies preparing descriptions in the context of a different language should replace instructions and guidelines prescribing or implying the use of English into their preferred language (see 4B3-4, 4B8-12, 4E, and areas 5 and 7).

VI. Spelling and style

DCRM(B) uses *Merriam-Webster's Collegiate Dictionary*, eleventh edition, as its authority in matters of spelling, and in matters of style, the fifteenth edition of the *Chicago Manual of Style*.

VII. Acronyms

AACR2	*Anglo-American Cataloguing Rules*, second edition
BDRB	*Bibliographic Description of Rare Books*
BIBCO	Monographic Bibliographic Program of the PCC
CC:DA	Committee on Cataloging: Description and Access, Association for Library Collections and Technical Services, American Library Association
DCRB	*Descriptive Cataloging of Rare Books*
DCRM	Descriptive Cataloging of Rare Materials
DCRM(B)	*Descriptive Cataloging of Rare Materials (Books)*
ISBD(A)	*International Standard Bibliographic Description for Older Monographic Publications (Antiquarian)*
LC	Library of Congress
LCRI	*Library of Congress Rule Interpretations*
PCC	Program for Cooperative Cataloging
RBMS	Rare Books and Manuscripts Section, Association of College and Research Libraries, American Library Association
RDA	*Resource Description and Access*

VIII. Examples and notes

VIII.1. Examples. The examples are not in themselves prescriptive, but are meant to provide a model of reliable application and interpretation of the rule in question. A word, phrase, element, or entire area may be illustrated; ISBD punctuation is given as needed only for the portion illustrated.

VIII.2. Notes. The instructions and guidelines in area 7 are written in imperative form. This does not imply that all notes are required; on the contrary, most notes are not (see 7A1.5). Consult the other areas of DCRM(B) in order to ascertain what is required and what is optional in any given situation (see 7A1). The conventions for notes included as part of the examples are as follows.

‣ *"Note"* indicates that the note is required if applicable to the situation.

‣ *"Optional note"* indicates that the note is not required. The labeling of a note as "optional" in these rules carries no judgment about its importance (see introductory section IV); certain notes designated as "optional" may in fact be almost universally applied.

‣ *"Local note"* indicates a note describing copy-specific information which is required if applicable to the situation (see 7B19).

‣ *"Optional local note"* indicates that the note concerns copy-specific information not affecting areas 1-6. It is not required, but must be clearly identified as a local note according to the provisions of 7B19.1.1. Copy-specific information that does affect areas 1-6, such as basing the description on an imperfect copy (see 0B2.2), is required and recorded in a general note.

‣ *"Comment"* prefaces details needed to adequately explain the example, and are not to be confused with notes appearing within the bibliographical description.

IX. Integrity of the copy

IX.1. Defects and sophistication

A greater vulnerability to damage, defect, and loss means that rare materials, especially older printed materials, are less likely than modern materials to be in a perfect or complete state when they reach the cataloger. One of the cataloger's tasks is to ascertain (within reasonable constraints) whether and how much the copy in hand deviates from its original state as issued. Imperfections and defects are usually easy to spot. Harder to spot during casual examination are replacement leaves, plates, or sections from another copy, and the cataloger is not expected to verify the integrity of each leaf in a publication unless there is reason to suspect that the copy in hand may have been made up, doctored, or falsified ("sophisticated"). Bibliographers' and booksellers' descriptions are the usual source of such information.

IX.2. Dust jackets

In the context of rare materials cataloging, dust jackets issued by the publisher are appropriately considered part of a publication, and are included in these rules as prescribed sources for areas 2, 4, and 6. Dust jackets often contain valuable information not found in any other source in the publication. Their easy detachability, however, coupled with their original function as protection for the binding only until it was safely in the hands of a reader, pose considerable difficulties for the rare materials cataloger. A fine dust jacket from a poor copy may have been exchanged with a poor dust jacket from a fine copy; the dust jacket of an original printing may end up on the copy of a later manifestation, and so on. When considering whether to transcribe information that appears only on a dust jacket, consider that the dust jacket was issued with the publication, unless there is reason to suspect otherwise.

X. Precataloging decisions

Before a bibliographic record can be created for a monograph or group of monographs awaiting cataloging in an institution's special collections, appropriate decisions must be made regarding the array of descriptive options available to the cataloger. These precataloging decisions include: determining whether DCRM(B) or AACR2 rules will govern the description, choosing the level of cataloging that will be applied, and determining the extent to which various options in the rules will be exercised.

Because DCRM(B) was written to address the special needs of users of rare materials, it is likely to be the appropriate cataloging code for the majority of printed monographs held in special collections. However, for some categories of materials, the cataloging objectives (see introductory section III) may be met by use of AACR2 or by the application of options within the DCRM(B) rules that permit less detail in the description. Full-level DCRM(B) records that employ all possible descriptive options will not necessarily be the best choice for every item.

The following section provides guidance for catalogers and cataloging administrators faced with these decisions and identifies some of the institutional and contextual factors that should be taken into consideration. It assumes that certain routine choices will already have been made, such as whether the encoding standard for the description will be MARC 21 and whether a resource issued as part of a monographic series or multipart monograph will be analyzed.

Institutions may promote efficiency by setting cataloging policies for specific categories of materials in their collections rather than making decisions on an item-by-item basis. For example, an institution may decide to catalog all pre-1831 books using DCRM(B), trace printers and booksellers for all pre-18th-century books, but give signature statements and expansive descriptive notes for 15th- and 16th-century books only. It may choose to catalog all later books according to AACR2, but add selected genre/form or provenance name headings. It may decide that collection-level cataloging is sufficient for brochures. A mechanism for easily making exceptions to general cataloging policy is desirable as well. If, for example, a curator buys a book for its notable cloth binding, description of and access to the binding ought to be given in the bibliographic record, even if it is not the institution's usual policy to describe bindings.

X.1. Decisions to make before beginning the description

X.1.1. Item-level vs. collection-level description

Determine whether the material will receive item-level description, collection-level description, or some combination of the two.

Item-level cataloging represents the normative application of the DCRM(B) rules. Guidelines for creating collection-level descriptions are found in Appendix B. Collection-level cataloging is usually faster than item-level—sometimes dramatically so—but is attended by such a substantial loss of specificity that its use as the sole final cataloging for a group of items should be chosen only after careful consideration. The lack of specificity can be mitigated through provision of some sort of item-level control, such as an inventory list, finding aid, or database, and such an approach is highly recommended. Collection-level cataloging of rare materials is most suitable when items have minimal value in themselves but derive value as part of a collection. Use of collection-level control by itself may be appropriate when users are unlikely to be seeking known items, or the risk of inadvertent purchase of duplicate individual items is considered insignificant. Collection-level control alone is unlikely to provide adequate evidence to identify materials following a theft.

A combination approach would entail individual cataloging of all or selected items in the collection in addition to the creation of a collection-level record. Such an approach may involve phased processing, whereby the cataloger creates a collection-level record to provide immediate basic access to the collection, and then later creates item-level records for priority items as time and resources permit.

X.1.2. Cataloging code: AACR2 vs. DCRM(B)

Determine which cataloging code will govern the description. Both codes contain optional rules in addition to the required ones, and each allows varying levels of cataloging depth.

In item-level bibliographic records, use of AACR2 results in a description that highlights the basic features of a publication and obscures some of the differences between manifestations or between variants of a single manifestation. AACR2 is generally considered to be easier and quicker to apply than DCRM(B). AACR2 is most suitable when, in an institutional context, an item was acquired and is of significance primarily for its content rather than its artifactual value. In contrast, use of DCRM(B) produces more faithful transcriptions and more accurate physical descriptions. It will be more likely to facilitate differentiation between manifestations and reveal the presence of bibliographic variants among seemingly identical items. DCRM(B) is most suitable when an item carries artifactual or bibliographical significance, or it is otherwise important to provide distinctions between issues, bibliographical variants, or individual copies.

X.1.3. Encoding level: DCRM(B) minimal vs. core vs. full

Determine whether the description will be done at a minimal, core, or full level. Each level has its particular uses with attendant advantages and disadvantages.

DCRM(B) minimal level provides for faithful transcription and exact physical description, but requires neither notes nor headings. Minimal-level records can be produced quite quickly. Because name and subject headings may be lacking, the materials represented by these records may be inaccessible through all but known-item searches, and so should be used only after careful consideration. DCRM(B) minimal level may be suitable when accurate physical description is desired but a record with few or no access points is acceptable, or when particular language expertise among current cataloging staff is insufficient for proper subject analysis. For further information on creating DCRM(B) minimal-level descriptions, see Appendix D.

DCRM(B) core level provides for faithful transcription and exact physical description, a full complement of name headings, and at least one subject heading, but requires few notes.[3] Core-level records may be suitable for items or collections that carry enough bibliographical or artifactual significance to benefit from detailed description and controlled heading access, but for which the omission of most notes is acceptable. For further information on creating DCRM(B) core-level descriptions, see Appendix C.

DCRM(B) full level represents the normative application of these rules, yet encompasses a range of potential levels of detail. Full-level records provide for faithful transcription and detailed, complete physical description. Although some notes are required (e.g., the source of the title proper if not the title page), most are optional and can be applied selectively depending on the nature of a collection or an institution's needs. For example, signature statements, descriptions of illustrative elements, names of illustrators and others responsible for such elements, and particular attributes of the item in hand may be included or omitted as desired.

Although treatment of headings is outside the scope of DCRM(B), full-level records typically contain a full complement of name and subject headings. In addition to those typically given to general materials, DCRM(B) full-level records may contain headings for printers, publishers, illustrators, engravers, former owners, binders, etc. The name headings need not be established using authority records, although full authority work, especially if contributed to the LC/NACO Authority File, will result in greater consistency of headings and improved access.[4]

The addition of genre/form headings is particularly encouraged in full-level records. These may be used to provide access by literary genre (e.g., Herbals, Booksellers' catalogs) or by physical form (e.g., Imposition errors, Annotations). Prefer terms found in the official thesauri maintained by the RBMS Bibliographic Standards Committee;[5] terms from other authorized thesauri (e.g., the *Art and Architecture Thesaurus*) may also be used as appropriate.

---

[3] If an institution is a BIBCO participant contributing core-level records as part of the Program for Cooperative Cataloging (PCC), all headings must be established in the LC/NACO and LC/SACO Authority Files.

[4] If an institution is a BIBCO participant contributing full-level records as part of the Program for Cooperative Cataloging (PCC), all headings must be established in the LC/NACO and LC/SACO Authority Files.

[5] These thesauri include: *Binding Terms*; *Genre Terms*; *Paper Terms*; *Printing and Publishing Evidence*; *Provenance Evidence*; and *Type Evidence*.

X.1.4. Bibliographic variants

If two or more items can be identified as bibliographic variants of an edition, decide whether to describe them using a single bibliographic record or multiple records.

It is taken as a default approach in DCRM(B) that a separate record will be made for each variant that represents what is referred to as an "edition" in AACR2 and an "issue" in bibliographic scholarship. However, this default approach is not prescriptive and indeed may not be desirable in every situation. Within the rules, alternatives are provided (see 2B3.2, 2B4.2, 2D2, 4G) that permit the creation of separate records for individual impressions, states, binding variants, or copies. Once the decision has been made to apply these alternative rules, the cataloger must be consistent in applying them to all areas of the description. For further guidance on the cataloging of bibliographic variants, see Appendix E.

X.2. Factors to consider in making these decisions

Consider the following factors when determining appropriate levels of description and access for materials awaiting cataloging. These factors will help to identify items that might deserve more detailed descriptions or higher priority treatment.

X.2.1. Institution's mission and user needs

Evaluate the relevance of the items awaiting cataloging to the institution's mission and the needs of its users. Ideally, the institution will have developed internal documentation that will facilitate such an evaluation, including a mission statement, collection development guidelines, and a listing of constituent users and their anticipated needs. The needs of both patrons (researchers, teachers, students, etc.) and staff (collection development, reference, technical services, etc.) should be taken into consideration.

X.2.2. Institutional and departmental resources

Evaluate institutional and departmental resources, especially staffing levels, expertise, and current workloads.

- ‣ Is staff able to keep up with the inflow of new materials?
- ‣ Is there a reasonable balance between resources devoted to acquiring materials and those devoted to processing them?

‣ Is current staff expertise in languages, subject areas, descriptive standards, and encoding standards adequate for implementing and/or completing proposed work plans?

‣ Is staff able to work concurrently with more than one code and/or description level?

‣ Are funding and space available for hiring new temporary or permanent staff with the necessary qualifications?

‣ Are adequate reference sources, such as specialized bibliographies, available for staff use?

‣ How many other projects are in process and what are their requirements and priorities?

The regular review of cataloging priorities is highly recommended and should include discussions with curatorial, public services, technical services, and preservation staff.

X.2.3. Market value and conditions of acquisition of the item or collection

Consider the conditions of acquisition and the estimated market worth of the item or collection awaiting cataloging.

‣ Does the monetary or public relations value of the material justify a higher level of access than would otherwise apply?

‣ Have any access requirements been imposed by a donor as part of the terms of acquisition?

‣ Is the item or collection accompanied by bibliographic descriptions that will facilitate cataloging?

X.2.4. Intellectual and physical characteristics of the item or collection

Finally, evaluate the intellectual and physical characteristics of the items awaiting cataloging.

‣ Is there a unifying characteristic that would justify and facilitate the description of the materials as a collection (e.g., author, publisher, place of publication, genre/form, etc.)?

‣ Is a particular collection renowned?

‣ Do the materials have a topical focus that has recently acquired importance or urgency (e.g., due to a scholarly conference hosted by the institution or the hiring of a new professor with a particular specialty)?

› Is cataloging copy generally available?

› Were the items purchased primarily for their content?

› Do the specific copies have bibliographic or artifactual value?

› Is the institution collecting deeply in the area?

› Are detailed descriptions likely to reveal bibliographic variants that will be of interest to researchers?

› Are detailed descriptions likely to help prevent the inadvertent purchase of duplicates or the failure to acquire desirable variants?

› Is the item or collection vulnerable to theft or vandalism?

› Would a more detailed description help prevent unnecessary handling by staff and researchers?

0. GENERAL RULES

Contents:
0A. Scope
0B. The basic description
0C. Chief source of information
0D. Prescribed sources of information
0E. Prescribed punctuation
0F. Language and script of the description
0G. Transcription

0A. Scope

These rules provide instructions for cataloging printed monographs—books, pamphlets, and single-sheet publications, other than maps and music—whose rarity, value, or interest make special description necessary or desirable. They cover instructions for the descriptive areas in bibliographic records only (see also introductory sections I-II). Individual and special issues of serials and unnumbered "special issues" may also be described as monographs (see Appendix H).

0B. The basic description

0B1. Required elements

The description must always include the following elements, regardless of the completeness of the information available:

- ‣ title proper
- ‣ date of publication
- ‣ extent
- ‣ size

Also include other elements of description as set out in the following rules, if available and appropriate to the chosen level of description.

0B2. Basis of the description

0B2.1. General rule. Base the description on the copy in hand.

0B2.2. Imperfect copies. If describing a copy known to be imperfect, and details of a perfect (or more perfect) copy can be determined, base the description on the perfect copy. Use square brackets only where required for description of the perfect copy. In such cases, the details may be determined by examining additional copies or by referring to reliable descriptions in other sources. As appropriate, cite the source used for the description in a note (see 7B3, 7B14). Make a local note describing the imperfection of the copy in hand (see 7B19.1).

If no reliable evidence of the details of a perfect copy is available, describe the copy as it is. Make a general note indicating that the description is based on an imperfect copy.

0C. Chief source of information

0C1. Single title page

0C1.1. The chief source of information for a publication other than a single sheet (see 1G) is the title page, or, if there is no title page, the source from within the publication that is used as a substitute for it. If information traditionally given on the title page is given on two facing pages or on pages on successive leaves, with or without repetition, treat all of these pages as the chief source of information.

0C1.2. However, if the publication bears a cover issued by the publisher, and the cover contains all the elements typically given on a title page but with more recent information than that provided on the title page (e.g., a later edition statement and publication date), choose the cover as the chief source of information. Make a note to indicate that the cover has been chosen as the chief source of information (see 7B3.1).

```
Poetry of animated nature illustrated : a chaste, interesting and
    instructive present for juveniles. -- Second edition. --
    Philadelphia : Published by Robert A. Smith, 1848
Note: Title, edition statement, and imprint taken from printed
    wrapper. Title page reads: Poetry of animated nature
    illustrated. In a series of numbers. Philadelphia: Published by
    Robert A. Smith, 1846
```

0C2. Multiple title pages

If the publication has more than one title page, choose as the chief source of information one of the following, applying the first applicable criterion:

a) If the title pages present the publication in different aspects (e.g., as an individual publication and as part of a multipart monograph), prefer the one that corresponds to the aspect in which the publication is to be treated.

b) If the publication is in more than one volume, each of which has a title page, use the title page in the first volume (or the lowest numbered volume if the first volume is not available).

c) If the publication is in one volume and the chief difference between multiple title pages is imprint date, choose the one with the latest date.

d) If the publication is in one volume and the chief difference between two title pages is that one is letterpress and the other is not, choose the letterpress title page.

e) If the publication has the same title page in more than one language or script, choose the title page that is in the language or script of the main part of the publication.

f) If two title pages face one another, choose the one on the recto of its leaf.

g) If two or more title pages follow one another, choose the first one.

Indicate in a note the source chosen as the chief source of information if other than the usual title page, or, in a multipart monograph, if other than the title page of the first volume (see 7B3).

0C3. No title page

For publications issued without a title page (and for publications issued *with* a title page when the title page is missing and no reliable description of it is available), if a single title proper is available in a single source within the publication, use this source as the title page substitute. If the same title proper is available in more than one source within the publication, choose as the title page substitute the source that supplies the most additional information. If different titles, or differing forms of the same title, appear within the publication, choose as the title page substitute one of the following, in this order of preference:

a) a source within the preliminaries or the colophon

b) a source elsewhere within the publication

c) a reference source

Indicate in a note the source chosen as the title page substitute (see 7B3).

Hereafter in these rules, "title page" means "title page or title page substitute."

0D. Prescribed sources of information

The prescribed source(s) of information for each area of the description is set out in preferred order below. Do not transcribe any information that is not present in the list of prescribed sources for that area.

Area	**Prescribed sources of information**
1. Title and statement of responsibility	Title page
2. Edition	Title page, other preliminaries, colophon, dust jacket (see introductory section IX.2)
3. Material (or type of publication) specific details	(Not applicable)
4. Publication, distribution, etc.	Title page, colophon, other preliminaries, dust jacket (see IX.2)
5. Physical description	The whole publication
6. Series	Series title page, monograph title page, cover,[6] dust jacket (see IX.2), rest of the publication
7. Note	Any source
8. Standard number and terms of availability	Any source

In all cases in which information for areas 1, 2, and 4 is taken from elsewhere than the title page, make a note to indicate the source of the information (see 7B3, 7B6, 7B7.1, 7B8). In all cases in which information for area 6 is taken from elsewhere than the series title page, make a note to indicate the source of the information (see 7B12).

The prescribed source of information for areas 1-6 of a single-sheet publication is the entire sheet, both recto and verso.

---

[6] Consider the cover to be a prescribed source only if it was issued by the publisher. Series-like statements present on covers not issued by the publisher usually represent binders' titles and should be treated as copy-specific information. They may be transcribed in a local note, if considered important. In case of doubt, do not consider the cover to be a prescribed source of information.

0E. Prescribed punctuation

Precede each area, other than the first, by a period-space-dash-space (. --) unless the area begins a new paragraph.

Precede or enclose each occurrence of an element of an area with standard punctuation as indicated in the "prescribed punctuation" sections in these rules.

Precede each mark of prescribed punctuation by a space and follow it by a space, with the following exceptions: the comma, period, closing parenthesis, and closing square bracket are not preceded by a space; the opening parenthesis and opening square bracket are not followed by a space.

End paragraphs with normal punctuation (usually the period).

If an entire area or element is omitted from the bibliographic description (e.g., because it is not present in the source), also omit its corresponding prescribed punctuation. Do not use the mark of omission.

0F. Language and script of the description

0F1. General rule

0F1.1. In the following areas, transcribe information from the publication itself in the language and script (wherever feasible) in which it appears there:

- Title and statement of responsibility[7]
- Edition
- Publication, distribution, etc.
- Series

0F1.2. Give interpolations into these areas in the language and script of the other information in the area, except for prescribed interpolations and other cases specified in these rules (e.g., 4B5, 4B6.2, 4C6.2). If the other information in the area is romanized, give interpolations according to the same romanization.

---

[7] If nonroman text has been transcribed within the first five words of the title proper, provide additional title access for a romanized form of the title proper (see Appendix F).

0F1.3. Give any other information (other than titles, citations, signatures, and quotations in notes) in the language and script of the cataloging agency.

0F2. Romanization

0F2.1. If it is not feasible to transcribe from the publication using a nonroman script, romanize the text according to the *ALA-LC Romanization Tables*. Do not enclose the romanized text within square brackets. Make a note to indicate that the romanized text appears in nonroman script in the publication (see 7B2.2).

> *Source*:
> ΔΙΟΝΥΣΙΟΥ ΟΙΚΟΥΜΕΝΗΣ περιήγησις
>
> *Transcription*:
> ```
> Dionysiou oikoumenēs periēgēsis
> Note: Title in Greek script
> ```
>
> *Source*:
> Hendecasyllabωn
>
> *Transcription*:
> ```
> Hendecasyllabōn
> Note: In the title, the ō in Hendecasyllabōn is printed in Greek
>       script
> ```

0F2.2. *Optionally*, if it is feasible to transcribe from the publication using a nonroman script, also provide parallel romanized fields using the *ALA-LC Romanization Tables*. Do not enclose the romanized text within square brackets, but indicate in a note that the romanization does not appear in the source.

> ```
> Note: Romanization supplied by cataloger
> ```

0G. Transcription

Transcribe information in the form and order in which it is presented in the source, according to these general rules 0B-0G, unless instructed otherwise by specific rules. Do not use the mark of omission to indicate transposition.

0G1. Letters, diacritics, and symbols

0G1.1. Letters and diacritics. In general, transcribe letters as they appear. Do not add accents and other diacritical marks not present in the source. Convert earlier forms of letters and diacritical marks to their modern form (see Appendix G2). In most languages, including Latin, transcribe a ligature by giving its component letters separately. Do not, however, separate the component letters of **æ** in Anglo-Saxon; **œ** in French; or **æ** and **œ** in ancient or modern Scandinavian languages. If there is any doubt as to the correct conversion of letters and diacritical marks to modern form, transcribe them from the source as exactly as possible.

0G1.2. Symbols, etc. Replace symbols or other matter that cannot be reproduced using available typographical facilities with a cataloger's description in square brackets. Make an explanatory note if necessary.

0G2. Capitalization and conversion of case

0G2.1. General rule. Convert letters to uppercase or lowercase according to the rules for capitalization in AACR2, Appendix A. Do not convert case when transcribing roman numerals.

0G2.2. Letters i/j and u/v. If the rules for capitalization require converting the letters **i/j** or **u/v** to uppercase or lowercase, follow the pattern of usage in the publication being described.[8] If the source uses a gothic typeface that does not distinguish between the letters **i/j** or the letters **u/v**, transcribe the letters as **i** and **v** respectively.

> *Source*:
> LES OEVVRES MORALES DE PLVTARQVE, TRANSLATEES DE GREC EN FRANÇOIS, REVEVES ET corrigees en plusieurs passages par le translateur
>
> *Transcription*:
> ```
> Les oeuures morales de Plutarque / translatees de grec en
>     françois, reueues et corrigees en plusieurs passages par le
>     translateur
> ```
> > (*Comment*: In the publication, the body of the text in roman type shows consistent use of v for vowels or consonants in initial position and u for vowels or consonants elsewhere, e.g., "ville," "vn," "conuersation," "tout," and "entendu")

---

[8] For information on early printing as it pertains to the transcription of **i/j** and **u/v**, and guidance on how to determine the pattern of usage, see Appendix G4. If any of the letters is transcribed within the first five words of the title proper in converted form, provide additional title access using alternative forms of the title proper as needed (see Appendix F).

0G2.3. Final capital "I" in Latin. Do not convert to lowercase a final capital **I** in Latin texts when the final **I** is uppercase and the immediately preceding letters in the word are lowercase or smaller capital letters. Since this usage is not merely typographic but affects meaning, the capital must be left in that form.[9]

Source:
M. AccI Plauti quae supersunt Comoediae

Transcription:
```
M. AccI Plauti quae supersunt Comoediae
```

0G2.4. Chronograms. Capital letters occurring apparently at random or in a particular sequence on a title page or in a colophon may represent a chronogram. Where there is good reason to assume that a chronogram is being used, do not convert letters considered part of the chronogram from uppercase to lowercase, or from lowercase to uppercase (see also 4D2.2).

0G3. Punctuation in the source

0G3.1. General rule. Do not necessarily transcribe punctuation as it appears in the source. Instead, follow modern punctuation conventions, using common sense in deciding whether to include the punctuation, omit it, replace it, or add punctuation not present.

Source:
The unhappy favourite; or, The Earl of Essex. A tragedy. Written by Jno;
    Banks

Transcription:
```
The unhappy favourite, or, The Earl of Essex : a tragedy /
    written by Jno. Banks
```

Source:
London: Printed for A Millar, over-against Catharine-street in the Strand.
    M,DCC,LI.

---

[9] If the letter occurs within the first five words of the title proper, provide additional title access for the form of title with the final capital **I** converted to **ii** (see Appendix F).

```
London : Printed for A. Millar, over-against Catharine-Street in
    the Strand, MDCCLI [1751]
```

Alternative rule: Transcribe all punctuation as found in the source of information, with the exception of those marks covered in rules 0G3.5-0G3.7. When following this alternative rule, always include prescribed punctuation as well, even if this results in double punctuation. Prescribed punctuation is treated at the beginning of each chapter within these rules.

```
The unhappy favourite; or, The Earl of Essex. : A tragedy. /
    Written by Jno; Banks
```
> (*Comment*: Commas are not required around *or* when applying this option; commas surrounding a conjunction introducing an alternative title are an AACR2 convention, not prescribed ISBD punctuation.

```
London: : Printed for A Millar, over-against Catharine-Street
    in the Strand., M,DCC,LI. [1751]
```

0G3.2. Apostrophes. Transcribe apostrophes as found. Do not supply apostrophes not present in the source.

```
Uncle Wiggly's picture book

Scotlands speech to her sons
```

0G3.3. Hyphens. Transcribe hyphens used to connect the constituent parts of compound words, normalizing their form as necessary (see Appendix G2). Do not supply hyphens not present in the source.

```
A catalogue of the library of Yale-College in New-Haven

Report of the Boston Female Anti Slavery Society
```

0G3.4. Punctuation within roman numerals. Do not transcribe internal marks of punctuation appearing within roman numerals. Omit them without using the mark of omission.

```
The bye-laws and regulations of the Marine Society, incorporated
    in MDCCLXXII
```

0G3.5. Ellipses, square brackets, and virgules. Do not transcribe ellipses ... or square brackets [ ] when present in the source; replace them with a dash -- and parentheses ( ) respectively or omit them, as appropriate. Do not confuse a virgule (/) in gothic typefaces with a slash; replace it with a comma or omit it, as appropriate. Make an explanatory note, if considered important.

> *Source*:
> Leominster, [Mass.]
>
> *Transcription*:
> ```
> Leominster, Mass.
> ```
> *Optional note*: `On t.p., "Mass." is enclosed by square brackets`

0G3.6. Line endings. Do not transcribe a hyphen or other mark of punctuation used to connect a single word divided between two lines; transcribe as a single word, ignoring the punctuation. If the function of the hyphen is in doubt (e.g., if it might form part of a compound word), transcribe it.

> *Source (showing line endings)*:
> I DISCORSI DI NICO-
> LO MACHIAVELLI, SO-
> PRA LA PRIMA DECA DI
> TITO LIVIO
>
> *Transcription*:
> ```
> I discorsi di Nicolo Machiauelli, sopra la prima deca di Tito
>     Liuio
> ```

0G3.7. Punctuation substituting for letters. Transcribe as hyphens any hyphens, dashes, or underscore characters used in the source as a substitute for one or more letters in a word or an entire word. Use one hyphen for each distinct piece of type.

> *Source*:
> Sec--t----s of st--te, the L----ds of the Ad------ty
>
> *Transcription*:
> ```
> Sec--t----s of st--te, the L----ds of the Ad------ty
> ```

Transcribe asterisks as asterisks.

```
par Mr. B***
```

If the values of the missing letters are known, provide the information in a note, if considered important.

Source:
Clara H_____d

Transcription:
```
Clara H-d
```
Optional note: Clara H-d is Clara Hayward

0G4. Spacing

0G4.1. Spacing within words and numbers. In general, follow modern spacing conventions when transcribing from the source. Make no attempt to preserve full or irregular spaces between letters within words. If a word is divided between the end of one line and the beginning of the next, transcribe it as a single word, ignoring the line-break.

Omit internal spaces when transcribing numbers (including roman numerals).

Source:
G R AE C AE GRAMMATICES

Transcription:
```
Graecae grammatices
```

Source (showing line endings):
DE LAVDI
BVS VRBIS ETRVRIAE
ET ITALIAE

Transcription:
```
De laudibus urbis Etruriae et Italiae
```

Alternative rule: Transcribe internal spaces within numbers (including roman numerals). If multiple spaces or different sizes of spaces appear between two characters within the number, transcribe them as a single space.

Source:
M. D. CC. XLIV

Transcription:
```
M. D. CC. XLIV
```

0G4.2. Spacing between words. If spacing between words in the source is ambiguous, or lacking, include spaces in the transcription to separate the words as needed.[10]

> *Source*:
> LAMORTE D'ORFEO

> *Transcription*:
> `La morte d'Orfeo`

0G4.3. Variant spellings. Do not insert spaces within single words that merely represent variant or archaic spellings.

> *Source*:
> Newhampshire & Vermont ALMANAC

> *Transcription*:
> `Newhampshire & Vermont almanac`

0G5. Omissions

0G5.1. General rule. Indicate omissions in the transcription or in a quoted note by using the mark of omission. When using the mark of omission, generally give it with a space on either side. However, give a space on only one side if the mark comes at the end of an area, is preceded by an opening parenthesis or opening square bracket, or is followed by a closing parenthesis, closing square bracket, or comma.

> `Oxford : Printed by Leon. Lichfield ... and are to be sold by the`
> `   Widow Howell, 1698`

> `Amsterdam : Printed for the Widow Swart ..., 1688`
> > (*Comment*: The mark of omission has a space on only one side because it is followed by a comma)

0G5.2. Information not considered part of any area. If omitting grammatically separable information from the transcription because it is not considered part of any area (pious invocations, etc.; see 1A2.2), do not use the mark of omission. If considered important, give the omitted information in a note.

---

[10] If the missing spaces occur in the first five words of the title proper, provide additional title access for the form of title as it appears in the source, without the spaces (see Appendix F).

0G5.3. Information not taken from the chief source of information. If transcribing information from a source other than the chief source of information, omit any words preceding or following the information if they are not considered part of the element and are grammatically separable. Do not use the mark of omission. If considered important, give the omitted text in a note.

```
The second edition
Note: Edition statement from colophon; full colophon reads: This,
    the second edition of Le morte Darthur, with Aubrey Beardsley's
    designs ... is limited to 1000 copies for the United Kingdom
    and 500 for America, after printing which the type has been
    distributed
```

0G6. Interpolations

0G6.1. General rule. Indicate an interpolation in the transcription or in a quoted note by enclosing it in square brackets. If transcribing text with missing or obscured letters or words that can be reconstructed with some certainty, include these in the transcription, enclosing them in square brackets.

```
amico[rum]
```
> (*Comment*: The word ends with a ⅄)

0G6.2. Conjectural and indecipherable text. Indicate a conjectural interpolation by adding a question mark immediately after the interpolation, within the square brackets. Supply a question mark enclosed in square brackets for each indeterminable word or portion of word. Make notes to justify the interpolations, provide explanations, or offer tentative readings of indecipherable portions of text, if considered important.

```
amico[rum?]
```
> (*Comment*: The word ends with a symbol of contraction that is conjectured to be a ⅄)

```
amico[?]
```
> (*Comment*: The symbol of contraction at the end of the word cannot be determined)

```
El[speth?] [?] McWhorter
```
> (*Comment*: An autograph with some conjectured letters in the forename and an indecipherable middle initial, transcribed in a local note)

0G6.3. Lacunae in imperfect copies. If the description is based on an imperfect copy (see 0B2.2), use the mark of omission enclosed in square brackets ([...]) to show lacunae in the resource.

```
En Barcelo[na] : Por Sebastian Mateu[...]
   Note: Description based on an imperfect copy; title page torn
      with partial loss of imprint
```

0G6.4. Blank spaces. If transcribing text containing a blank space intended to be completed in manuscript, as is common in forms and certain government documents, supply the word "blank" enclosed in square brackets.[11] If the blank has been completed in the item being described, indicate this in a local note, if considered important.

```
A catalogue of books, to be sold on [blank] the [blank] day of
   February, 1755 ...
   Optional local note: Library's copy has date of auction supplied
      in manuscript: [Wednesday] the [26th] day of February, 1755
```

0G6.5. Adjacent elements within a single area. If adjacent elements within one area are to be enclosed in square brackets, generally enclose them in one set of square brackets.

```
[Leipzig : W. Stürmer], 1572
```

If the square brackets are due to interpolations such as corrections or expansions (see 0G8.2, 4B3, 4B4, 4B5), however, use separate pairs of square brackets.

```
Lugduni [Lyon] : [Philippe Tighi?], 1573
```

0G6.6. Adjacent elements in separate areas. If adjacent elements are in different areas, enclose each element in a set of square brackets.

```
At London : Imprinted for VVilliam Aspley, [1613] -- [48], 418 p.
```

0G7. Misprints, etc.

0G7.1. Misprints. Transcribe a misprint as it appears in the publication. Follow such an inaccuracy either by "[sic]" or by the abbreviation "i.e." and the correction within square brackets.[12]

```
Of the knowledeg [sic] whiche maketh a wise man
```

---

[11] If the blank occurs in the first five words of the title proper, provide additional title access for the form of title without the interpolated word "[blank]" (see Appendix F).

[12] If the misprint occurs in the first five words of the title proper, provide additional title access for the form of title without the interpolation and for the form of title as if it had been printed correctly (see Appendix F).

LEEDS METROPOLITAN UNIVERSITY LIBRARY

```
The notted [i.e. noted] history of Mother Grim

One day's dty [i.e. duty]
```

Do not correct words spelled according to older or non-standard orthographic conventions, e.g., "françoise" for "française," or "antient" for "ancient."

0G7.2. Turned and approximated letters. Transcribe a turned letter (i.e., a letter set upside-down), whether inadvertent or deliberate, as the intended letter. Transcribe two letters used to approximate a third letter as the intended letter. However, transcribe **vv** as **vv** (see Appendix G5). Make an explanatory note, if considered important.[13]

```
London
Optional note: First "n" in "London" printed with a turned "u"

Wittenberg
Optional note: The "W" in "Wittenberg" is formed using "rv"
```

0G7.3. Blank spaces for initial letters. When the printer has left a blank space for an initial letter, supply the intended letter in square brackets, regardless of whether the letter has been executed in manuscript, and make an explanatory note. If a guide letter has been printed, transcribe it without square brackets. In case of doubt about whether a printed guide letter is present, transcribe the letter without square brackets. Make a local note to indicate the presence or absence of manuscript execution in the copy, if considered important.

```
[H]istoriarum libri XXXV
Note: Space for initial letter of first word of title left blank
   by printer
Optional local note: LC copy: Initial letter executed in red and
   green ink

Historiarum libri XXXV
Optional local note: LC copy: Printed guide letter "H" at
   beginning of title not executed in manuscript
```

---

[13] If the two letters used to approximate a third letter occur in the first five words of the title proper, provide additional title access for the form of title with the letters transcribed as set (see Appendix F).

0G8. Abbreviations and contractions

0G8.1. When transcribing from the publication, do not abbreviate any words not abbreviated in the source.

0G8.2. If special marks of contraction have been used by the printer in continuance of the manuscript tradition, expand affected words to their full form and enclose supplied letters in square brackets (see Appendix G3). Make an explanatory note, if considered important (see 7B4.2). If a contraction standing for an entire word appears in the source, supply instead the word itself, enclosed in square brackets. However, transcribe an ampersand or a Tironian sign (⁊) as an ampersand. Enclose each expansion or supplied word in its own set of square brackets.

```
Esopus co[n]structus moralizat[us] & hystoriatus ad vtilitate[m]
    discipulo[rum]
```

If the meaning of a contraction is conjectural, apply the bracketing conventions given in 0G6.2.

0G9. Superscripts and subscripts

Transcribe superscript and subscript characters on the line unless the sense would be affected (e.g., in a mathematical formula).

Source:
Mr J.^{as} McAdam

Transcription:
```
Mr. Jas. McAdam
```

0G10. Initials, etc.

0G10.1. Transcribe initials, initialisms, and acronyms without internal spaces, regardless of how they are presented in the source of information.

```
Pel battesimo di S.A.R. Ludovico ...

KL Ianuarius habet dies xxxi

Monasterij B.M.V. Campililioru[m]

J.J. Rousseau
```

0G10.2. Treat an abbreviation consisting of more than a single letter as if it were a distinct word, separating it with a space from preceding and succeeding words or initials.

```
Ph. D.

Ad bibliothecam PP. Franciscan. in Anger

Mr. J.P. Morgan
```

0G10.3. If two or more distinct initialisms (or sets of initials), acronyms, or abbreviations appear in juxtaposition, separate them with a space.

```
M. J.P. Rabaut
```
　　　　(*Comment*: The first initial stands for Monsieur)

1. TITLE AND STATEMENT OF RESPONSIBILITY AREA

Contents:

1A. Preliminary rule

1A1. Prescribed punctuation

For instructions on the use of spaces before and after prescribed punctuation, see 0E.

Precede the title of a supplement or section (see 1B6) by a period.

Precede each parallel title by an equals sign.

Precede each unit of other title information by a colon.

Precede the first statement of responsibility by a diagonal slash.

Precede each subsequent statement of responsibility by a semicolon.

For the punctuation of this area when a publication has no collective title, see 1F.

1A2. Sources of information

1A2.1. General rule. The prescribed source of information for the title and statement of responsibility area is the title page. For special provisions relating to single-sheet publications, see 1G.

1A2.2. Omission of pious invocations, etc. Omit, without using the mark of omission, information found on the title page that constitutes neither title information nor a statement of responsibility. Such information may include pious invocations, quotations, devices, announcements, epigrams, mottoes, prices, etc. (see 0G5.2). Transcribe or describe this kind of information in a note if it is considered important. If such information is a grammatically inseparable part (see 1B1) of one of the elements of the title and statement of responsibility area, however, transcribe it as such. If such information constitutes the only title-like information present in the source, it may be used as a devised title according to the provisions of 1B5.

1A2.3. Multipart monographs. If the volume is part of a multipart monograph, and the title page gives a statement of the volume or part number within the larger work, omit this statement without using the mark of omission, unless it is a grammatically inseparable part (see 1B1, 1B4) of the information being transcribed. Do transcribe statements such as "in two volumes," however (see 1D3).

1A3. Form and order of information

Transcribe title and statement of responsibility information in the form and order in which it is presented in the source, unless instructed otherwise by specific rules (see 0G).

1B. Title proper

1B1. Words considered part of the title proper

1B1.1. The title proper is the first element of the description. Title information preceding the chief title on the title page is considered part of the title proper. If the chief title is preceded or followed in the source by other elements of information, transpose these elements to their appropriate areas in the description (or give them in a note) unless case endings would be affected, the grammatical construction of the information would be disturbed, or the text is otherwise grammatically inseparable from the title proper. In the latter cases, transcribe the information as part of the title proper.

```
The post-humous works of Robert Hooke

Monsieur Bossu's treatise of the epicke poem

M. Tullii Ciceronis de officiis libri tres

Bell's edition of Shakspere
```

1B1.2. Make a note to indicate the original position on the title page of transposed elements.

```
Prudence Palfrey : a novel / Thomas Bailey Aldrich
Note: Author's name at head of title
```

1B2. Note on the source of the title proper

Make a note on the source of the title proper if it is a title page substitute, e.g., the caption title, docket title, etc.

```
A new list of fifty two ships sent to the East-Indies
Note: Docket title
```

1B3. Forms of the title proper

The title proper can take a variety of forms, some of which are exemplified below:

1B3.1. Title proper inclusive of other titles or other title information appearing before the chief title on the title page:

```
Seculum Davidicum redivivum, The divine right of the revolution
    scripturally and rationally evinced and applied
```
> (*Comment*: By virtue of its typographical prominence, the English title is clearly the chief title)

```
Prize dissertation, which was honored with the Magellanic Gold
    Medal, by the American Philosophical Society, January, 1793.
    Cadmus, or, A treatise on the elements of written language
```
> (*Comment*: "Cadmus …" is clearly more prominent than "Prize dissertation …")

```
Hereafter foloweth a litel boke called Colyn Cloute
```
> (*Comment*: "Colyn Cloute" is the chief title)

1B3.2. Title proper inclusive of alternative titles:

```
Christianographie, or, The description of the multitude and
    sundry sorts of Christians in the vvorld not subject to the
    Pope
```

1B3.3. Title proper consisting solely of the name of a responsible person or body:

```
Salustius
```

1B3.4. Title proper inclusive of a caption. (See 1G4 for caption titles on single-sheet publications):

> *Source*:
>
> To the Honourable Commissioners appointed by Act of Parliament for enquiring into the Losses and Services of the American Loyalists. The memorial of Silvester Gardiner humbly sheweth, ...

> *Transcription*:
> ```
> To the Honourable Commissioners appointed by act of Parliament
>     for enquiring into the losses and services of the American
>     loyalists. The memorial of Silvester Gardiner humbly sheweth
>     ...
> ```

1B4. Title proper with grammatically inseparable designation

If a publication is in more than one volume and the title proper of each volume includes a grammatically inseparable designation such as numbering that is specific to that volume, supply in square brackets after the first designation a hyphen and the final designation, omitting intermediate designations. Do the same for single-volume publications that contain multiple parts.

```
Quinti Horatii Flacci epistolarum liber primus[-secundus]

Thomas Masterson his first[-second] booke of arithmeticke

Le premier[-quart] volume de messire Jehan Froissart lequel
    traicte des choses dignes de memoire aduenues tant es pays de
    France, Angleterre, Flanders, Espaigne que Escoce, et autres
    lieux circonuoisins
```

If it is not feasible to do this, transcribe the title proper of the first volume or part without this interpolation and make a note about the later designation(s).

1B5. No title proper

If no title can be found in any source, use as the title proper the opening words of the text if these provide a reasonably distinctive title. If the opening words of the text are not suitable, or if the beginning of the text is lacking, devise a brief descriptive title, preferably in the language and script of the cataloging agency, and use this devised title, enclosed in square brackets, as the title proper. Indicate in a note whether the title proper is taken from the opening words of the text or has been devised by the cataloger.

```
I am a jolly huntsman, my voice is shrill and clear
```
Note: Title from opening two lines of poem

> (*Comment*: Title is not bracketed because the first page of text is here the title page substitute)

```
[Observations on a bill relative to the militia]
```
Note: Title devised from content

> (*Comment*: Opening words "Herewith and the desire of being serviceable in the smallest degree to my country ..." not suitable as title)

```
[Sermon on Christian baptism]
```
Note: Title devised from content of sermon

1B6. Title proper with supplementary or section designation or title

If the title proper for a work that is supplementary to, or a section of, another work appears in two or more grammatically separable parts, transcribe the title of the main work first, followed by the designation(s) and/or title(s) of the supplement(s) or section(s) in order of their dependence. Separate the parts of the title proper by periods. If the arrangement indicated requires transposition, make a note to indicate the actual reading of the titles.

```
Faust. Part one
```
Note: Title page reads: Part one. Faust

If describing an individual issue of a serial, transcribe the numbering of the issue as instructed in Appendix H.

1B7. Abridgments of the title proper

1B7.1. General rule. Abridge a long title proper only if it can be done without loss of essential information. Do not omit any of the first five words. Indicate omissions by the mark of omission.

```
An act or law passed by the General Court or Assembly of His
    Majesty's English colony of Connecticut ... on the seventh day
    of February ... 1759
```

1B7.2. Alternative title. If the title proper contains an alternative title, do not omit any of the first five words of the alternative title.

```
England's alarm, or, A most humble declaration, address, and
    fervent petition ...
```

1B7.3. Chief title. Extend the transcription of the title proper through to the end of the chief title of the resource. Apply this provision even if other words in the title proper precede the chief title (see 1B1.1, 1B3.1). If the end of the chief title cannot be determined, break off the transcription at the first grammatically acceptable place, but in no event within the first five words of the chief title.

```
Jo. Danielis Schoepflini consil. reg. ac Franciae historiogr.
   vindiciae typographicae
```
> (*Comment*: The chief title is "Vindiciae typographicae")

```
A brand new song, entitled The Irishman's address to the twenty-
   six Nottingham worthies ...
```
> (*Comment*: The chief title begins "The Irishman's address" but its ending is ambiguous)

1C. Parallel titles

1C1. Order and source of parallel titles

Transcribe parallel titles in the order indicated by their sequence on, or by the layout of, the title page. If the original title appears elsewhere than on the title page, transcribe it in a note, if considered important.

1C2. Language of parallel titles and relationship to title proper

1C2.1. Transcribe an original title in a language different from that of the title proper appearing on the title page as a parallel title, unless it is grammatically inseparable from another part of the description.

```
Fables = Fabulae
```

1C2.2. Transcribe as other title information an original title in the same language as the title proper (see 1D).

```
The adventures of Red Riding Hood : Little Red Riding Hood
```

1D. Other title information

1D1. Order and source of other title information

Transcribe other title information appearing on the title page in the order indicated by the sequence on, or layout of, the title page. Transcribe other title information not appearing on the title page in a note, if considered important.

1D2. Other title information beginning with prepositions, conjunctions, etc.

1D2.1. General rule. Transcribe title information that appears following the title proper as other title information, even if it begins with a preposition, conjunction, prepositional phrase, etc.

```
The English Parliament represented in a vision : with an after-
   thought upon the speech delivered to His Most Christian Majesty
   by the deputies of the states of Britany on the 29th day of
   February last ... : to which is added at large the memorable
   representation of the House of Commons to the Queen in the year
   1711/12 ...
```

1D2.2. If this other title information appears following the statement of responsibility, transcribe it as a subsequent statement of responsibility (see 1E14.2).

1D2.3. If this other title information, or some portion of it, constitutes a formal statement of the contents of the work, and is grammatically separable from the title proper and other title information, transcribe it in a note, if considered important (see 7B16.2). When these formal statements are omitted from the title and statement of responsibility area, use the mark of omission.

```
The spinning wheel's garland : containing several excellent new
   songs ...
Optional note: Contents: (from t.p.) I. The good housewife's coat
   of arms -- II. The spinning wheels glory -- III. The taylor
   disappointed of his bride -- IV. The changeable world
```

1D2.4. Distinguish the above situations from those in which titles of other works are given equal prominence with the first-named work (see 1F1).

1D3. Statements about illustrations or volumes

Treat an illustration statement or a statement such as "in two volumes" as other title information, unless the statement is grammatically inseparable from information transcribed as part of another element or area (see 1E13 and 2B8). If the statement appears following the statement of responsibility, transcribe it as a subsequent statement of responsibility.

```
The American child's pictorial history of the United States :
   illustrated by sixty engravings

General index to fifty-six volumes of the Gentleman's magazine :
   from its commencement in the year 1731 to the end of 1786 /
```

```
compiled by Samuel Ayscough, clerk, assistant librarian of the
British Museum ; in two volumes
```

1D4. Abridgment of other title information

Optionally, if other title information is very lengthy and can be abridged without loss of essential information, omit less important words or phrases, using the mark of omission. If considered important, transcribe omitted words or phrases in a note (including the other titles or phrases referred to in 1D2.3).

1D5. Other title information with grammatically inseparable elements

If the other title information includes a statement of responsibility or an element belonging to another area, and the element is a grammatically inseparable part of the other title information according to one or more of the conditions enumerated in 1B1.1, transcribe it as other title information.

```
Constitutiones legitime seu legative regionis Anglicane : cu[m]
    subtilissima interpretatione Johannis de Athon
```
> (*Comment*: Statement of responsibility transcribed as part of other title information because of genitive case ending)

1D6. Parallel statements containing other title information

Transcribe parallel statements containing other title information in the order in which they appear on the title page.

1E. Statements of responsibility

1E1. Statements of responsibility on the title page

Transcribe statements of responsibility found on the title page in the form in which they appear.

```
The history of the long captivity and adventures of Thomas
    Pellow, in South-Barbary ... / written by himself

De indiciis et praecognitionibus : opus apprime utile medicis /
    Dauide Edguardo Anglo authore

I dieci libri di architettura / di Leon Battista Alberti

Thoughts on education / by the late Bishop Burnet

Moore's Irish melodies / illustrated by D. Maclise, R.A.
```

1E2. Statements of responsibility on other sources

If a statement of responsibility appears in a source other than on the title page, or is taken from outside the publication, record the statement and its source in a note.

> *Note*: `Pref. signed: Thomas Hopkins`
> (*Comment*: Hopkins is not recorded in the statement of responsibility area even though he is known to be the author)

> *Note*: `"By an engineer"--Introd.`

1E3. Transposition of statements of responsibility

If a statement of responsibility precedes the title proper in the source, transpose it to its required position unless it is a grammatically inseparable part of the title proper according to one or more of the conditions enumerated in 1B1.1. When transposing the statement of responsibility, do not use the mark of omission. Make a note indicating the transposition.

> `Hanc dissertationem medicam de hydrope tympanite ... submittit ad`
> `   diem [blank] Martii MDCLXXII ... David Richter, Zittâ-Lusatus,`
> `   autor / praeside ... Dn. Johanne Arnoldo Friderici`
> *Note*: `"Praeside" statement precedes title on t.p.`

1E4. Single statements of responsibility with two or more names

1E4.1. Transcribe a single statement of responsibility as such whether the two or more persons or corporate bodies named in it perform the same function or different functions.

> `Puzzled people : a study in popular attitudes to religion,`
> `   ethics, progress, and politics in a London borough / prepared`
> `   for the Ethical Union by Mass-Observation`

> `A new method of discovering the longitude both at sea and land`
> `   ... / by William Whiston and Humphry Ditton`

> `A treatise of health and long life, with the sure means of`
> `   attaining it : in two books / the first by Leonard Lessius, the`
> `   second by Lewis Cornaro ...`

1E4.2. If a respondent and praeses are given for an academic disputation, treat both names and the words indicative of their function as part of a single statement of responsibility (unless grammatically inseparable from the title proper or other title information).

```
      / pro disputatione publica proponebatur praeside Jacobo Fabricio,
          respondente Johanne Reembbelt
```

```
  but De peripneumonia disputationem ... sub praesidio ... Dn. Jacobi
        Fabricii ... publice examinandam proponit Johannes Hellinger
```

1E5. Omission of names in statements of responsibility

When a single statement of responsibility names more than one person or corporate body performing the same function or with the same degree of responsibility, transcribe all the names mentioned. *Optionally*, if the responsible persons or bodies named in a single statement are considered too numerous to list exhaustively, all after the third may be omitted. Indicate the omission by the mark of omission and supply "et al." in square brackets.

```
      / collected by the long practice, experience, and pains of J.H.,
          Esquire, Matthew Hodson, Mr. Holled ... [et al.]
```

1E6. Two or more statements of responsibility

If there are two or more statements of responsibility, transcribe them in the order indicated by their sequence on, or by the layout of, the title page. If the sequence and layout are ambiguous or insufficient to determine the order, transcribe the statements in the order that makes the most sense.

```
  El Fuero Real de España / diligentemente hecho por el noble Rey
      don Alonso noveno ; glossado por Alonso Díaz de Montalvo ...
```

1E7. Terms of address, etc., in statements of responsibility

Include titles and abbreviations of titles of nobility, address, honor, and distinction that appear with names in statements of responsibility.

```
  / by Horatio Walpole, Earl of Orford ...
```

```
  / par Monsieur Guilliaulme Staundforde, chiualer
```

```
  / by the late Sir Thomas Fitzosborne, bart. ...
```

```
  / con un prólogo del Excmo. Sr. D. Manuel Danvila y Collado
```

```
  / by the Rev. Daniel Lysons ...
```

1E8. Qualifications in statements of responsibility

Qualifications such as initials indicating membership in societies, academic degrees, and statements of positions held may be omitted from the statement of responsibility, using the mark of omission, unless:

> the qualifications are necessary grammatically

> *or*   the qualifications are necessary for identifying the person or are useful in establishing a context for the person's activity (initials of religious orders, phrases, or adjectives denoting place names, etc.)

> *or*   the statement of responsibility represents the author only by a pseudonym, a descriptive phrase, or nonalphabetic symbols.

1E9. Ambiguous statements of responsibility

If the relationship between the title of a work and the person(s) or body (bodies) named in the statement of responsibility is not clear, supply an explanatory word or short phrase in the language of the text, within square brackets, or make a note.

```
De l'humour noir / [compilé par] André Breton
```

If considered important, make notes about expansions, explanations, and corrections of statements of responsibility when needed for clarity (see 7B6).

1E10. Statements of responsibility and more than one language or script

1E10.1. If there are titles in more than one language or script, but only a single statement of responsibility, transcribe the statement of responsibility after all the title information.

```
Jeux de cartes pour enfants = Children's playing cards / par
    Giovanni Belgrado et Bruno Munari
```

1E10.2. If there are both titles and statements of responsibility in more than one language or script, transcribe each statement of responsibility after the title proper, parallel title, or other title information to which it relates. If any of these titles lack a matching statement of responsibility, transcribe the information in the order indicated by the sequence on, or by the layout of, the title page.

```
Anatomia uteri humani gravidi tabulis illustrata / auctore
    Gulielmo Hunter ... = The anatomy of the human gravid uterus
    exhibited in figures / by William Hunter
```

1E10.3. Make a note to indicate the original position on the source of any transposed statements.

1E11. Nouns and noun phrases

1E11.1. Treat a noun or noun phrase occurring in conjunction with a statement of responsibility as other title information if it is indicative of the nature of the work.

```
Comus : a mask / by John Milton
```

1E11.2. If the noun or noun phrase is indicative of the role of the person(s) or body (bodies) named in the statement of responsibility rather than of the nature of the work, treat it as part of the statement of responsibility.

```
Paradise lost : a poem in twelve books / the author John Milton

A cushion of downe / text by Gilbert Frye ; drawings by Charles
    Cox

Life and adventures of Valentine Vox, the ventriloquist / with
    illustrations by Phiz
```

1E11.3. In case of doubt, treat the noun or noun phrase as part of the statement of responsibility.

1E12. Persons or bodies not explicitly named in statements of responsibility

Transcribe a statement of responsibility as such even if no person or body is explicitly named in that statement. Such statements will generally contain words like "translated," "edited," "compiled," etc.

```
The folovving of Christ / translated out of Latin into English
```

1E13. Statements of responsibility with grammatically inseparable elements

If the statement of responsibility includes information belonging to another area, and the information is grammatically inseparable from the statement of responsibility according to one or more of the conditions enumerated in 1B1.1, transcribe it as part of the statement of responsibility.

```
L'hymne au soleil / traduit en vers latins, sur la troisième
     édition du texte françois, par M. l'abbé Métivier
```

1E14. Phrases about notes, appendixes, etc.

1E14.1. Transcribe phrases about notes, appendixes, and such accompanying matter in the order indicated by the sequence on the title page. If such information appears before the statement of responsibility, transcribe it as other title information (see 1D2.1).

```
Chemische Erfahrungen bey meinem und andern Fabriken in
     Deutschland : nebst einem Anhang besonderer chemischer
     Geheimnisse / von J.A. Weber

Clarion call : with Franklin Phelps' criticisms / by Lunceford
     Yates
```

1E14.2. If such information appears after the statement of responsibility, transcribe it as a subsequent statement of responsibility, whether or not it names a person or body.

```
High life below stairs : a farce / by James Townley ; with a
     variety of German notes explanatory of the idioms ... alluded
     to by John Christian Huttner

Some remarks on the Barrier Treaty, between Her Majesty and the
     States-General / by the author of The conduct of the allies ;
     to which are added the said Barrier-Treaty ; with the two
     separate articles ...

Monsieur Bossu's treatise of the epick poem ... / done into
     English from the French, with a new original preface upon the
     same subject, by W.J. ; to which are added An essay upon Satyr
     by Monsieur d'Acier ; and A treatise upon pastorals by Monsieur
     Fontanelle
```

1E14.3. *Optionally*, if the phrases are very lengthy and can be abridged without loss of essential information, omit less important words or phrases, using the mark of omission. If considered important, transcribe omitted phrases in a note. If the phrases are actually titles of other works given equal prominence with the title of the first work, see 1F.

1F. Publications without a collective title

1F1. Two or more works named on the title page

1F1.1. By same person or body. If the publication has no collective title and the title page bears the titles of two or more individual works, other than supplementary matter, that are contained in the publication, transcribe the titles of the individual works in the order in which they appear on the title page. Separate the titles by a space-semicolon-space if the works are all by the same person(s) or body (bodies), even if the titles are linked by a connecting word or phrase.

```
Les Akanças : prologue mélo-dramatique, en un acte et en prose ;
    suivi Des Espagnols dans la Floride : pantomime en trois actes
    et à spectacle
```

1F1.2. By different persons or bodies. If the individual works are by different persons or bodies, or the authorship is in doubt, precede each title other than the first by a period and one space, unless a linking word or phrase is already present. Precede each statement of responsibility by a space-slash-space.

```
The serving-man become a queen. Jockey of the green. The lass of
    Richmond Hill
```

```
Franklin's way to wealth and Penn's maxims
```

1F2. One or more works not named on the title page

If the publication has no collective title, and one or more works contained in the publication are not named on the title page:

transcribe the title and statement of responsibility from the title page, and name the other work(s) in a contents note (see 7B16)

or   make a separate description for each separately titled work, linking the separate descriptions with "With" notes (see 7B18)

or   devise a collective title for the whole publication, preferably in the language and script of the cataloging agency, and use this devised title, enclosed in square brackets, as the title proper

```
[Acts of Parliament enacted in 1732]
```

1G. Single-sheet publications

1G1. Chief source of information

The chief source of information for single-sheet publications is the whole sheet, recto and verso.

1G2. General rule

In general, transcribe the information presented beginning with the first line of printing. If the printing is arranged in columns with no information preceding the body of the text, begin the transcription with the top line of the extreme left column (extreme right column in the case of languages that are read right to left). Retain in the transcription dates, addresses, and other information necessary for identification. Use judgment, but in case of doubt, start the transcription with the first words of printed text on the sheet. If the initial text is grammatically independent of the succeeding material and is one of the following, however, begin the transcription after it without using the mark of omission:

‣ caption to an illustration

‣ copyright statement

‣ device

‣ edition statement

‣ publication, distribution, etc., statement

‣ motto

‣ official numbering

‣ page number

‣ part of an illustration or ornament

‣ price

‣ tabular material

If the initial text has been omitted, indicate the nature and position of the omitted material in a note, if considered important.

1G3. Chief title

If there is a word or phrase obviously intended as the chief title of the publication that is not the first line of printing, transcribe it as the entire title proper, omitting information appearing before it on the page without the mark of omission. In general, apply this instruction only when such a title is not integrated grammatically with the rest of the text, is set off typographically, and has as its sole function the naming of the piece as a whole. When such a title is selected, also give in a note at least the first five words of the first line of printing as described above. In case of doubt as to the selection of the chief title, start the transcription with the first line as described above.

1G4. Caption title

If a caption title is present, normally transcribe this title in full. If there is no caption title, transcribe the text as found at least until a relatively distinctive word or phrase is included. If the distinctive word or phrase is not near the beginning of the transcription, less important words or phrases preceding it may be omitted, using the mark of omission. Do not, however, abridge the transcription before the sixth word. If the text is very lengthy, end the transcription at the first grammatically acceptable place after the caption title or the distinctive word or phrase; the omitted material may be summarized in a note, if considered important.

1G5. Prescribed punctuation

Information transcribed from single-sheet publications usually does not lend itself to the application of the punctuation prescribed in 1A1 for the title and statement of responsibility area. If, however, the information can be separated clearly and unmistakably into title proper, other title information, or statement of responsibility without any transposition, supply the prescribed punctuation.

1G6. Two or more works with a collective title

If there are two or more works printed on a single sheet having a collective title, transcribe only the collective title as the title proper. Make a formal or informal contents note for the works.

1G7. Two or more works without a collective title

If there are two or more works printed on a single sheet that does not have a collective title, transcribe as the title statement the first title or opening words of the text. Make a formal or informal contents note and include in it the titles of the additional works. If the sheet is printed on both sides and it is impossible to determine which side should be read first, make a separate bibliographic record for each side of the sheet, and include a formal "With, on verso" note in each record (see 7B18).

1G8. Two or more works with separate publication, distribution, etc., statements

If there are two or more works printed on a single sheet and each has its own publication, distribution, etc., statement, or there is other conclusive evidence that they were intended to be separately issued, make a separate bibliographic record for each work that was intended to be issued separately. Include a formal "With" note in each record (see 7B18) indicating that the works were printed on a single sheet and that they were "intended to be separated." If there are two or more works printed on a single sheet giving the appearance that they were possibly intended to be separated, but there is no conclusive evidence that this is the case, follow the provisions of 1G7, and include a note indicating that they were "possibly intended to be separated."

2. EDITION AREA

Contents:

2A. Preliminary rule

2A1. Prescribed punctuation

For instructions on the use of spaces before and after prescribed punctuation, see 0E.

Precede the edition area by a period-space-dash-space.

Precede a statement relating to a named revision of an edition by a comma.

Precede the first statement of responsibility following an edition statement by a diagonal slash.

Precede each subsequent statement of responsibility by a semicolon.

For the use of the equals sign to precede parallel statements, see the appropriate rules following.

2A2. Sources of information

The prescribed sources of information for the edition area are the title page, other preliminaries, colophon, and dust jacket (see introductory section IX.2), in that order of preference. If an edition statement or any part of the edition area is transcribed from elsewhere than the title page, indicate its source in a note.

```
The third edition corrected, and considerably enlarged
Note: Edition statement from half-title

Book Club edition
Note: Edition statement from dust jacket
```

2A3. Form and order of information

Transcribe edition information in the form and order in which it is presented in the source, unless instructed otherwise by specific rules (see 0G).

2B. Edition statement

2B1. General rule

Transcribe a statement relating to an edition or issue of a publication as it appears, according to the general rules 0B-0G. Include any explanatory words or phrases appearing with the edition statement.

2B2. Words considered part of the edition statement

2B2.1. Edition statements normally include either the word "edition" (or its equivalent in other languages), or a related term such as "revision" or "issue."

```
The second edition

Cinquiesme édition, reueuë, corrigée, & augmentée

Nunc primum in lucem aedita

Editio secunda auctior et correctior
```

2B2.2. Treat a phrase such as "newly printed" as an edition statement unless it is part of a statement being transcribed in the publication, distribution, etc., area. In case of doubt, treat such a statement as an edition statement.

```
Newly imprinted and very necessary vnto all youthe
```
       (*Comment*: But transcribe a statement such as "Philadelphia printed, London reprinted" in the publication, distribution, etc., area rather than the edition area)

2B3. Words such as "impression" or "printing"

2B3.1. Use judgment in transcribing statements containing words such as "impression" or "printing." In books from the hand-press era, such statements usually signal a new edition or issue. In these cases, the statement may properly be considered an edition statement.

```
The second impression

A new printing
```

2B3.2. In books from the machine-press era, statements containing words such as "impression" or "printing" are more likely to indicate that the publication is simply a new impression of the same edition. Omit statements of impression such as these from the transcription without using the mark of omission. Local notes may be made about the statements, if considered important.

> *Optional local note*: Library's copy has "ninth printing" on t.p.
>   verso

Alternative rule: If a decision has been made to create a separate bibliographic description for an individual impression, state, binding variant, or copy within a single edition or issue (see introductory section X.1.4 and Appendix E), transcribe statements containing words such as "impression" or "printing" in the edition area. Indicate the source of the statement, if other than the title page, in a note.

> Ninth printing
> *Note*: The words "ninth printing" taken from t.p. verso

2B4. Edition statements with special characters or a numeric emphasis

2B4.1. If an edition statement consists entirely or chiefly of characters that are neither numeric nor alphabetic, transcribe the characters as they appear if the necessary typographical facilities are available. For characters that cannot be reproduced, substitute the names or descriptions of the characters in square brackets.

> &&& edition

> [alpha chi] edition

2B4.2. If an edition statement consists of one or more letters or numbers without accompanying words, or only words that convey numbers, supply an appropriate word or abbreviation in square brackets. If no appropriate word or abbreviation can be determined, or in cases of doubt, simply transcribe the statement as found.

> 3e [éd.]

> Second [ed.]

If such a statement signals a substantially unchanged impression of an edition, omit it from the transcription without using the mark of omission. Local notes may be made about such statements, if considered important.

```
Optional local note: Library's copy: "Fifth ten thousand"

Optional local note: Library's copy: Number "2" on t.p. indicates
    2nd printing

Optional local note: Library's copy: "51st-100th"--T.p. verso

Optional local note: Library's copy: "163-173 Tausend"

Optional local note: Library's copy: Number line on t.p. verso
    indicates 3rd printing: "8 7 6 5 4 3 88 89 90 91 92"

Optional local note: Library's copy: Publisher's code "B-O" on
    t.p. verso indicates printed Feb. 1914; see Boutell, H.S. First
    editions (4th ed., rev. and enl.)
```

Alternative rule: If a decision has been made to create a separate bibliographic description for an individual impression, state, binding variant, or copy within a single edition or issue (see introductory section X.1.4 and Appendix E), transcribe statements such as the following in the edition area, even if they represent a substantially unchanged impression of that edition: a statement consisting entirely or chiefly of characters that are neither numeric nor alphabetic; a statement consisting of one or more letters or numbers without accompanying words; or a statement consisting only of words that convey numbers. Supply appropriate words or abbreviations in square brackets, as needed. Indicate the source of the statement, if other than the title page, in a note.

```
51st-100th
Note: The words "51st-100th" taken from t.p. verso
```

If identification of the substantially unchanged impression is based on a publisher's code or number line or on information found in a reference source, supply an appropriate statement in square brackets, as needed. Indicate the basis for the statement in a note.

```
[3rd printing]
Note: Number line on t.p. verso indicates 3rd printing: "8 7 6
    5 4 3 88 89 90 91 92"
```

2B5. No edition statement

2B5.1. If the publication does not contain an edition statement, but is known to contain significant changes from other editions, or an edition statement for it is provided by a reference source, do not supply an edition statement based on this information. Give the information in a note.

> *Note*: "Sixth ed."--Tchemerzine, v. 6, p. 117-131

2B5.2. If the publication contains only a statement that refers to another edition (e.g., as part of a preface to an earlier edition or a summary of the work's publication history), do not transcribe the information as an edition statement and do not supply an edition statement based on the information. Notes may be made on such statements, if considered important.

> *Optional note*: "Preface to the first edition": p. 5-7
> (*Comment*: The publication is not the first edition)

2B6. Edition statements that are grammatically inseparable parts of other areas

If an edition statement is a grammatically inseparable part of another area according to one or more of the conditions enumerated in 1B1.1, and has been transcribed as such, do not repeat it as an edition statement.

> Old New York, or, Reminiscences of the past sixty years : being
>   an enlarged and revised edition of the anniversary discourse
>   delivered before the New York Historical Society ...
>
> Chirurgia / nunc iterum non mediocri studio atque diligentia a
>   pluribus mendis purgata

2B7. Transposition of edition statements

Transpose grammatically separable edition statements into the edition area from other parts of the title page. Provide details of the transposition in a note.

2B8. Edition statements with grammatically inseparable information

If information pertaining to other elements of the description (e.g., an original title or other information concerning the original work) is grammatically inseparable from the edition statement according to one or more of the conditions enumerated in 1B1.1, transcribe it as part of the edition statement. If illustration statements or statements such as "in two volumes" appear with an edition statement, transcribe them as they appear (see also 1D3).

2B9. Edition statements in more than one language or script

2B9.1. If the publication bears edition statements in more than one language or script, transcribe the statement that is in the language or script of the title proper. If this criterion does not apply, transcribe the statement that appears first in the source. Transcribe the remaining statement(s), together with any associated statements of responsibility, as parallel edition statements. Precede each parallel statement by an equals sign. Make a note to indicate the original position on the source of any transposed statements.

2B9.2. *Optionally,* if it is considered that the parallel statements are too numerous to list exhaustively, and that some may be omitted without significant loss of identification, omit parallel statements after the first using the mark of omission. Transcribe the omitted statement(s) in a note, if considered important.

2B10. Two or more works on the title page with at least one edition statement

If the title page bears the titles of two or more individual works contained in the publication, and one or more of these works has an edition statement associated with it, transcribe each edition statement in the title and statement of responsibility area along with the title to which it pertains.

```
An examination of Dr. Burnet's theory of the earth ... / by J.
    Keill, The second edition corrected ... To the whole is annexed
    A dissertation on the different figures of coelestial bodies,
    &c ... / by Mons. de Maupertuis
```

2B11. Edition statements on multipart monographs

2B11.1. If cataloging a multipart monograph, and the edition statement varies or does not appear on all of the volumes, ascertain whether the set was issued as such. If the publication was issued as such, base the transcription on the first volume and make a note to indicate variation in, or absence of, the edition statements in the subsequent volumes. In case of doubt, assume the set was not issued as such.

```
Revised edition
Note: Vol. 2 issued without the edition statement
```

2B11.2. If the multipart monograph is known or assumed to be a made-up set (assembled from different editions by an owner) and reliable descriptions of the editions are available, make separate descriptions for each edition. In each description, make a local note indicating that the set is imperfect and identifying which volumes are wanting.

```
Second edition
Local note: Library's copy imperfect: v. 2 wanting; a previous
    owner has supplied v. 2 from the 3rd ed. to create a made-up
    set
```
   (*Comment*: The first of two descriptions associated with the made-up set)

```
Third edition
Local note: Library's copy imperfect; v. 1 wanting; a previous
    owner has supplied v. 1 from the 2nd ed. to create a made-up
    set
```
   (*Comment*: The second of two descriptions associated with the made-up set)

2B11.3. If the multipart monograph is known or assumed to be a made-up set and reliable descriptions of the editions are not available, base the description on the copy in hand. Make a note to indicate that the description is based on a made-up set.

```
First edition
Note: Description based on a made-up set; v. 3 has "second
    edition"
```

2C. Statements of responsibility relating to the edition

2C1. General rule

2C1.1. Transcribe a statement of responsibility relating to one or more editions, but not to all editions, of a given work following the edition statement if there is one. Such statements may include the reviser or illustrator of a new edition, or a corporate body responsible for a new edition. Follow the instructions in 1E for the transcription and punctuation of such statements of responsibility.

```
The second edition / with notes of various authors by Thomas
    Newton
```

2C1.2. Do not, however, apply this provision to such statements that do not name or otherwise identify a person or corporate body.

```
    The second edition revised and corrected

not The second edition / revised and corrected
```

2C1.3. In determining the extent of the edition statement and the beginning of the statement of responsibility relating to the edition, it may be necessary to take into account the layout, punctuation, and typography of the title page as well as the sense of the text. Such words as "Revised and enlarged," when appearing with the name of a person or body, might be transcribed either as part of the edition statement or as part of the statement of responsibility relating to the edition, depending on their presentation on the title page.

2C2. Transposition of statements of responsibility not relating to the edition

If a statement of responsibility appears after the edition statement, transpose it to the title and statement of responsibility area in all cases except when it clearly applies only to the edition being cataloged. Make a note to indicate this transposition.

```
An inquiry into the original state and formation of the earth :
   deduced from facts about the laws of nature / by John
   Whitehurst. -- The second edition, considerably enlarged, and
   illustrated with plates
Note: The statement "by John Whitehurst" appears on the t.p.
   after the edition statement
```
   (*Comment*: Statement of responsibility applies to all editions)

2C3. Phrases about notes, appendixes, etc.

2C3.1. If there are phrases about notes, appendixes, and such supplementary matter and they apply to the edition in hand but not necessarily to all editions of the work, transcribe them as statements of responsibility relating to the edition only in the case when the phrase names or otherwise identifies a person or corporate body and appears in the same source as the edition statement.

```
The fourth edition / with a new epilogue by the author

Editio altera, ab innumeris erroribus emendata / huic editioni
   accessere Jacobi Bongarsii excerptiones chronologicae ad
   Justini historias accommodatae
```

2C3.2. If the phrase does not name a person or corporate body, transcribe it as part of the edition statement proper or as part of the first statement of responsibility relating to the edition, as appropriate. Do not introduce the semicolon (as in 1E14.2) to separate such phrases from preceding statements of responsibility.

```
The fourth edition, with notes

A new edition / by Grace Webster, to which is added a life of the
   author
```

2C3.3. If such phrases have been transposed from a position preceding the edition statement, provide details of the transposition in a note.

2C4. Statements of responsibility relating to the edition in more than one language or script

2C4.1. If the publication has parallel edition statements (see 2B9) but a statement of responsibility relating to the edition in only one language or script, transcribe the statement of responsibility after all the edition statements.

2C4.2. If the publication has parallel edition statements (see 2B9) and statements of responsibility relating to the edition in more than one language or script, transcribe each statement of responsibility after the edition statement to which it relates.

2C4.3. Make a note to indicate the original position on the source of any transposed statements of responsibility.

2D. Statement relating to a named revision of an edition

2D1. If the publication is a named revision of an edition, transcribe the statement relating to that revision as instructed in 2B.

> The third edition, Reprinted with a new preface
>   (*Comment*: Statement indicates the publication is a revision of the third edition)

2D2. Do not transcribe a statement relating to a reissue of an edition if it represents a substantially unchanged impression of that edition. Omit the impression statement without using the mark of omission. Local notes may be made about such statements, if considered important.

> The second edition
> *Optional local note*: Library's copy is "The fifth impression"

> *Alternative rule*: If a decision has been made to create a separate bibliographic description for an individual impression, state, binding variant, or copy within a single edition or issue (see introductory section X.1.4 and Appendix E), transcribe a statement relating to a reissue of an edition, even if it represents a substantially unchanged impression of that edition, in the edition area. Indicate the source of the statement, if other than the title page, in a note.
>
> ```
> The second edition, The fifth impression
> Note: "The fifth impression" taken from the t.p. verso
> ```

2E. Statements of responsibility relating to a named revision of an edition

2E1. Transcribe a statement of responsibility relating to a named revision of an edition following the statement relating to the revision.

```
Third edition, The second revision / with considerable additions
    and an appendix by George Wither
```

2E2. Transcribe such statements of responsibility according to the applicable provisions of 2C.

3. MATERIAL (OR TYPE OF PUBLICATION) SPECIFIC DETAILS AREA

No general use of this area is made for printed monographs.

4. PUBLICATION, DISTRIBUTION, ETC., AREA

Contents:
4A. Preliminary rule
4B. Place of publication, distribution, etc.
4C. Name of publisher, distributor, etc.
4D. Date of publication, distribution, etc.
4E. Place of manufacture
4F. Name of manufacturer
4G. Date of manufacture

4A. Preliminary rule

4A1. Prescribed punctuation

For instructions on the use of spaces before and after prescribed punctuation, see 0E.

Precede this area by a period-space-dash-space.

Precede a second or subsequently named place of publication, distribution, etc., by a semicolon, unless a linking word or phrase is given in the publication.

Precede the name of the first publisher, distributor, etc., by a colon. Precede the name of a second and any subsequent publisher, distributor, etc., by a colon, unless a linking word or phrase is given in the publication.

Precede the date of publication, distribution, etc., by a comma.

Enclose the details of manufacture (place, name, date) within parentheses.

Precede a second or subsequently named place of manufacture by a semicolon, unless a linking word or phrase is given in the publication.

Precede the name of the first manufacturer by a colon. Precede the name of a second and any subsequent manufacturer by a colon, unless a linking word or phrase is given in the publication.

Precede the date of manufacture by a comma.

For the use of the equals sign to precede parallel statements, see the appropriate rules following.

4A2. Sources of information

4A2.1. The prescribed sources of information for the publication, distribution, etc., area are the title page, colophon, other preliminaries, and dust jacket (see introductory section IX.2), in that order of preference. If the information for an element is not present in these sources, any source may be used to supply needed information (see 0G6). If statements belonging to different elements are found in separate sources, combine them to make a complete statement in the publication, distribution, etc., area. However, do not combine statements belonging to a single element when they appear in different sources within the publication.

4A2.2. If any part of the publication, distribution, etc., area is taken from a source other than the title page, make a note to indicate the source (see 7B8). Make a note about information not transcribed in the publication, distribution, etc., area, if it is considered important.

4A3. Form and order of information

4A3.1. Transcribe publication, distribution, etc., information in the form and order in which it is presented in the source, unless instructed otherwise by specific rules (see 0G).

4A3.2. If statements belonging to different elements appear out of order, or as part of another area, and they are grammatically separable, transpose them as needed. Make a note indicating the original position of the transposed elements.

```
Mexico : Imprenta de la Escalerillas dirigida por Manuel Ximeno,
    1828
Note: Date follows place of publication in imprint

Philadelphia : Published by Johnson & Warner, 1813
    ([Philadelphia] : William Greer, printer)
Note: Printer precedes date of publication on t.p.

[Jena] : Verlegt zu Jena von Joh. Jacob Ehrdten, anno 1698
    ([Mühlhausen] : Gedruckt zu Mühlhausen von Tobias David
    Brücknern)
Note: Printer statement appears before date on t.p.
```

4A3.3. If the elements are not grammatically separable, or their transposition would result in an ambiguous or otherwise confusing construction, transcribe them in the order found and supply missing elements in square brackets as needed (see 0G6).

> [London] : Emprynted the yere of oure Lorde a. MCCCCC & xiij by Richard Pynson, prynter vnto the kyng[es] noble grace, [1513]
> (*Comment*: The date of publication has not been transposed because it is not a grammatically separable element)

4A4. Fictitious or incorrect information

If all information relating to the publication, distribution, etc., area appearing in the publication is known to be fictitious or incorrect, transcribe it nonetheless. If the real details are known, or can be reasonably surmised, supply them at the end of the area as a correction in square brackets. Give the source of this information in a note. If some but not all of the information is known to be fictitious or incorrect, apply the appropriate rule (see 4B9, 4C5, 4D2.4).

> Sadopolis : Chez Justin Valcourt ... à l'enseigne de la Vertumalheureuse, an 0000 [i.e. Brussels : Jules Gay, 1866]
> *Note*: Corrected imprint from: Pia, P. Livres de l'Enfer

4A5. Information covered by labels, etc.

If any of the original details relating to the publication, distribution, etc., area are covered by a label or other means showing later information, transcribe the later information. If the original details are visible or otherwise available, transcribe or give them in a note.

4A6. Elements relating to publication, distribution, etc., vs. elements relating to manufacture

Consider the wording, layout, and typography of the publication itself when determining the most appropriate place to transcribe information relating to the publication, distribution, etc., area. Keep in mind that statements relating to printing will sometimes be more appropriately transcribed as elements of publication, distribution, etc., and sometimes as elements of manufacture.[14] Consult the following instructions for guidance.

4A6.1. Statements relating to publication, distribution, etc., only

If the publication bears only a statement relating to publication, distribution, etc., or multiple such statements, transcribe the statement(s) according to the instructions in 4B, 4C, and 4D.

```
Geneuae : Sumptibus Petri Chouët, 1651

Viennae : Impensis Joannis Pauli Kraus, bibliopolae Viennensis,
    1768

New-York : Sold by D. Felt & Co. ; Boston : Published by Cha's
    Ellms, agent, [1835?]
```

4A6.2. Statements relating to manufacture only

4A6.2.1. If the publication bears only a statement relating to manufacture, or multiple such statements, generally assume the manufacturer(s) to also be functioning as publisher(s), distributor(s), etc. Transcribe the statement(s) according to the instructions in 4B, 4C, and 4D. Consider the words "place of publication" and "publisher" in those instructions to refer equally to the place of manufacture and name of manufacturer in such cases.

```
Moguntiae : In typographeio Ioannis Albini, anno 1602

Edmonton : Jas. E. Richards, government printer, 1907

Te Philadelphia : Gedrukt bij Hendrik Miller, in de Twede Straat,
    MDCCLXII [1762]

Albany : Printed by Websters and Skinners ; New-York :
    Stereotyped by G. Bruce, 1822
```

---

[14] The roles of publishers, printers, and booksellers were not clearly delimited in the hand-press period. Statements relating to printing frequently appear prominently on early printed materials, reflecting the tendency of printers to function as more than solely manufacturers. As the book trade industry became increasingly specialized over time, however, the role of the publisher gradually assumed greater importance, while the roles of manufacturer and distributor came to be subordinate.

4A6.2.2. However, if the manufacturer is known not to be the publisher, distributor, etc., and the identity of the publisher, distributor, etc., can be determined or reasonably surmised, supply the name of the publisher, distributor, etc., in square brackets and transcribe the manufacturer statement as such according to the instructions in 4E, 4F, and 4G.

```
[Boston : New York & Erie Railroad Company, 1856] (Boston :
    Farwells & Forrest, steam job printers, 5 Lindall Street)
```

4A6.3. Statements relating both to publication, distribution, etc., and to manufacture

If the publication bears statements relating both to publication, distribution, etc., and to manufacture, determine whether or not the statements are grammatically separable.

4A6.3.1. If the statements are grammatically inseparable, transcribe them according to the instructions in 4B, 4C, and 4D. Consider the words "place of publication" and "publisher" in those instructions to refer equally to the place of manufacture and name of manufacturer in such cases.

```
Boston : Printed by Robert Hodge, for Nathaniel Coverly, in
    Newbury-Street, [1782]

[Westzaandam] : Gedrukt voor den uitgever by H.J. de Roode te
    Westzaandam, en zyn te bekomen te Amsteldam by B. van der Klok,
    boekverkooper op de Blaauw Burgwal, 1765

Germantown, in Pennsylvania : Printed by Christopher Sower and
    sold in Charles-Town, South-Carolina, by Jacob Viart, book-
    seller in Elliot Street, [1757]
```

4A6.3.2. If the statements are grammatically separable, determine which statement is emphasized in the source, whether typographically (larger font size, uppercase letters, boldface, etc.) or by appearing first.

4A6.3.2.1. If a manufacturer statement has been emphasized, transcribe all of the statements according to the instructions in 4B, 4C, and 4D. Consider the words "place of publication" and "publisher" in those instructions to refer equally to the place of manufacture and name of manufacturer in such cases.

```
Londini : Typis H. Parker : Cura Josephi Pote, bibliopolae
    Etonensis, 1732
```

```
Oppenheimio : Ex officina typographica Hieronymi Galleri :
    Sumptibus Johannis Theodori de Bry, 1617

Manchester : Printed at the office of G. Nicholson, No. 9,
    Spring-Gardens ; London : Sold by T. Knott, No. 47, Lombard-
    Street and Champante & Whitrow, Jewry-Street, 1796
```

4A6.3.2.2. If a publisher, distributor, etc., statement has been emphasized, transcribe the publisher, distributor, etc., statement(s) according to the instructions in 4B, 4C, and 4D and transcribe the manufacturer statement(s) according to the instructions in 4E, 4F, and 4G.

```
Boston : Published by William Parker, 1816 (Brookfield [Mass.] :
    E. Merriam & Co., printers)

Tot Middelburgh : By Zacharias Roman, boeck-vercooper ..., anno
    1636 (Tot Middelburgh : Gedruckt by Hans vander Hellen ...)

New York : Livermore & Rudd, 1856 ([New York] : Electrotyped by
    Thomas B. Smith, 82 & 84 Beekman Street : Printed by J.D.
    Torrey, 18 Spruce Street)
```

4B. Place of publication, distribution, etc.

4B1. General rule

4B1.1. Transcribe the names of places associated with publishers, distributors, and booksellers as part of this element. Transcribe the names of places associated with printers and other manufacturers only if appropriate according to the instructions in 4A6 (i.e., when the wording, layout, or typography of the publication suggests that the manufacturer is also functioning as the publisher, distributor, etc.).

4B1.2. Transcribe the place of publication, distribution, etc., as it appears in the source. If the place appears together with the name of a larger jurisdiction (e.g., country, state, or similar designation), or multiple such jurisdictions, transcribe this as well.

```
Elizabeth-Town

Köln

Apud inclytam Germaniae Basileam

Commonwealth of Massachusetts, Boston

Saskatoon, Saskatchewan, Canada
```

4B2. Places of publication, distribution, etc., with initial prepositions, etc.

Include in the transcription any prepositions appearing before the place of publication, distribution, etc., as well as any accompanying words or phrases associated with the place name.

```
A Lyon

In London

In Boston, printed
```
>   (*Comment*: Title page reads: "In Boston, printed. 1705." Following provisions of 4D1.3, "printed" is here transcribed with the place)

```
Printed at Bennington

Impressum fuit hoc opus Venetiis
```

4B3. Supplied modern forms of place names

If considered necessary for identification and if known, supply in square brackets the modern form of the name of the place. Use an English form of the name, if there is one.

```
Christiania [Oslo]

Eboracum [York]

Monachii [Munich]
```
> *but* `Madridii`
>   (*Comment*: Recognizable as "Madrid" without qualification)

4B4. Supplied fuller forms of place names

If a place name is found only in an abbreviated form in the source, transcribe it as found. Supply in square brackets the full form of the name, or the remainder of the name, if considered necessary for identification.

```
Mpls [i.e. Minneapolis]

Rio [de Janeiro]
```

4B5. Supplied larger jurisdictions

Supply in square brackets the name of the country, state, province, etc., after the name of the place if it is considered necessary for identification, or if it is considered necessary to distinguish the place from others of the same name. Use a modern English form of the name, if there is one. Apply the abbreviations appearing in AACR2, Appendix B.

```
Cambridge [England]

Newport [R.I.]

Washington [Pa.]
```

4B6. Two or more places of publication, distribution, etc.

4B6.1. If the source of information shows two or more places and all are related to the same publisher, distributor, etc., transcribe all in the order in which they appear.

```
London ; York

A Lausanne & se trouve à Paris
```

4B6.2. *Optionally*, if it is considered that the places are too numerous to list exhaustively, and that some may be omitted without significant loss of identification, the place of publication, distribution, etc., statement may be shortened by omitting all the places after the third. In such cases, use the mark of omission and supply after it in square brackets a phrase in the language and script of the cataloging agency to convey the extent of the omission. Include the number of omitted places (if more than one) in the supplied phrase.

```
London ; Reading ; Bath ... [and 6 other cities in England]
```

4B6.3. If a subsequent place of publication, distribution, etc., is not related to the same publisher, distributor, etc., transcribe it in association with the publisher, distributor, etc., to which it corresponds.

```
New York : Ivison, Phinney, and Co. ; London : Trübner & Co.
```

4B6.4. Do not, however, transcribe a subsequent place as a place of publication, distribution, etc., if it must be recorded as a grammatically inseparable part of another element.

```
Printed at Worcester, Massachusetts : By Isaiah Thomas : Sold by
   him in Worcester, by said Thomas and Andrews in Boston, and by
   said Thomas and Carlisle, in Walpole, Newhampshire
```

4B6.5. If a place of publication, distribution, etc., associated with an earlier edition appears together with the actual place of publication, distribution, etc., of the edition being described, transcribe the places as a single element in the order in which they appear.

```
Philadelphia printed, London reprinted
```

4B6.6. If both the place and publisher, distributor, etc., associated with an earlier edition appear together with the place and publisher, distributor, etc., of the edition being described, transcribe each place with the publisher, distributor, etc., to which it corresponds.

```
London : Printed for Knight and Lacy, Paternoster-Row ;
   Greenfield, Mass. : Re-printed by Ansel Phelps, and for sale by
   him at his bookstore, also by West & Richardson, Cummings,
   Hilliard & Co., Boston, and Wilder & Campbell, New-York
```

4B7. Places of publication, distribution, etc., in multipart monographs

If the publication is issued in more than a single physical part, and the place of publication, distribution, etc., changes in the course of publication, give the place of publication, distribution, etc., of the later part(s) in a note.

```
Stuttgart ; Tübingen
Note: Place of publication in v. 33-40: Stuttgart ; Augsburg
```

4B8. Place names that are grammatically inseparable parts of other areas, etc.

If the place of publication, distribution, etc., appears only as a grammatically inseparable part of another area and is transcribed there, or appears only as a grammatically inseparable part of the publisher, distributor, etc., statement and is transcribed there, supply in square brackets the place of publication, distribution, etc., as the first element of the publication, distribution, etc., area (see 4C3). Use a modern English form of the name, if there is one.

```
[Munich] : Durch Peter Clement, Kunstführer zu München
```

4B9. Fictitious or incorrect places of publication, distribution, etc.

If the place of publication, distribution, etc., appearing in the publication is known to be fictitious or incorrect, supply a correction in square brackets, using a modern English form of name, if there is one, and give the basis for the correction in a note. If, however, the entire statement consisting of place, publisher, and date is known to be fictitious or incorrect, apply 4A4.

```
Londres [i.e. Paris]
Note: Actual place of publication from: Weller, E.O.  Falsche
   Druckorte
```

4B10. No place of publication, distribution, etc.

4B10.1. If no place of publication, distribution, etc., appears in the publication, supply one in square brackets. Use a modern English form of the name, if there is one, and include the name of the larger jurisdiction if considered necessary for identification. Use the location associated with the first transcribed publisher, distributor, etc., if one is present. Provide a justification for the supplied place in a note if necessary.

```
[Cambridge, Mass.] : Printed by Samuel Green, 1668
Note: Samuel Green was located in Cambridge, Mass., from 1660 to
   1672
```

4B10.2. If the name of the place has changed over time, supply the name appropriate to the date of publication, distribution, etc., if known (e.g., Leningrad, not St. Petersburg, for works published in that city between 1924 and 1991). If considered necessary for identification, also supply the modern place name and the name of the larger jurisdiction.

```
[Christiania i.e. Oslo]

[Leona Vicario i.e. Saltillo, Coahuila, Mexico]
```

4B11. Place of publication, distribution, etc., supplied based on address or sign

Supply in square brackets the name of the place of publication, distribution, etc., using a modern English form of the name, if there is one, when only an address or sign appears in the publication. (Transcribe the address or sign as the publisher, distributor, etc., statement; see 4C4.1) When supplying the place, give a justification in a note if necessary.

```
[Paris]
```
   (*Comment*: Imprint reads: "à l'enseigne de l'éléphant," the trade sign of a Parisian printer)

```
[London]
```
   (*Comment*: Imprint reads: "sold in St. Paul's Church Yard")

4B12. Place of publication, distribution, etc., uncertain or unknown

4B12.1. If the place of publication, distribution, etc., is uncertain, supply the name of the probable place of publication, distribution, etc., with a question mark, using a modern English form of the name, if there is one, all in square brackets.

```
[Amsterdam?]

[Newport, R.I.?]

[St. Petersburg?]
```

4B12.2. If no city of publication, distribution, etc., can be conjectured, supply the name of a state, province, country, or other larger geographic entity as the place of publication, distribution, etc., with a question mark if necessary, using a modern English form of the name, if there is one, all in square brackets.

```
[Canada]

[Surrey?]

[Prussia?]

[South America?]
```

4B12.3. If the reason for supplying the place is not apparent from the rest of the description, make a note to indicate the source of the information.

```
Note: Place of publication suggested by Alden
```

4B12.4. If no place of publication, distribution, etc., can be supplied, use the abbreviation "s.l." (sine loco) in square brackets.

```
[S.l.]
```

4B13. Place names in more than one language or script

4B13.1. If the name of the place of publication, distribution, etc., appears in more than one language or script, transcribe the statement in the language or script of the title proper, or if this criterion does not apply, transcribe the statement that appears first. Transcribe the remaining statement(s) as parallel statements, preceding each by an equals sign. Make a note to indicate the original position on the source of any transposed statements.

4B13.2. *Optionally*, if it is considered that the parallel statements are too numerous to list exhaustively, and that some may be omitted without significant loss of identification, omit parallel statements after the first using the mark of omission. Transcribe the omitted statement(s) in a note, if considered important.

4C. Name of publisher, distributor, etc.

4C1. Transcribe the names of publishers, distributors, and booksellers as part of this element. Transcribe the names of printers and other manufacturers only if appropriate according to the instructions in 4A6 (i.e., when the wording, layout, or typography of the publication suggests that the manufacturer is also functioning as the publisher, distributor, etc.).

4C2. Transcribe the name of the publisher, together with any preceding words or phrases, as it appears in the publication.

```
: Em caza de Guilherme Strahan

: Printed, and re-printed by E. Waters

: In the Flete Strete in the sygne of the Sonne by Wynkyn de
  Worde

: Imprimerie d'E. Duverger, rue de Verneuil, no 4
```

Optionally, omit addresses and insignificant information in the middle or at the end of the publisher, distributor, etc., statement, unless the information aids in identifying or dating the publication or is deemed important to the cataloging agency (e.g., for the purpose of capturing book trade data). Indicate all omissions by the mark of omission.

```
: Chez Testu, imprimeur-libraire ... Blanchon, libraire ... et
  les marchands de nouveautés
```

If a statement such as "Privately printed" appears on the title page, transcribe it as, or as part of, the publisher, distributor, etc., statement.

```
: Privately printed
```

4C3. Publisher, distributor, etc., statements containing grammatically inseparable place names or dates

If the publisher, distributor, etc., statement contains grammatically inseparable statements relating to place or date of publication, distribution, etc., transcribe the information as part of the publisher, distributor, etc., element. Supply the place or date of publication, distribution, etc., in square brackets in the appropriate element (see 4B8, 4D1.4; see also 4A3.3).

```
[London] : Printed in the year of our Lord 1665 for the author
    Lodowick Muggleton, in Great Trinity-Lane London, near the sign
    of the Lyon and Lamb, [1665]
```

4C4. Publisher, distributor, etc., statements containing only addresses, signs, or initials

4C4.1. If only the address, sign, or initials of the publisher, distributor, etc., appear in lieu of the name, transcribe the statement containing the address, sign, or initials as the publisher, distributor, etc., statement (see also 4B11). If the publisher's, distributor's, etc., name can be identified, supply it in square brackets after the initials or before or after the address or sign, as appropriate, or give the information in a note.

```
: Printed for W.W. [i.e. William Welby] and are to be solde in
    Paule's Church yarde at the signe of the Grey-hound
Note: Bookseller's name identified in STC (2nd ed.)

: Printed for I.T.
Note: Printed by Miles Flesher for John Trundle; see STC (2nd
    ed.)

: [Jean-Pierre Costard] rue Saint-Jean-de-Beauvais, la premiere
    porte cochere au dessus du College
Note: Costard listed as printer in Quérard

: Ad insigne Pinus [i.e. Hans Schultes, the Elder]
Note: Colophon: Augustae Vindel. Ex officina typographica
    Iohannis Praetorii, anno MDCI. Praetorius was a latinized form
    used by Hans Schultes in some imprints; see Benzing, J.
    Buchdrucker (1982 ed.)
```

4C4.2. If the identification of the publisher, distributor, etc., is based on a device, supply the name of the publisher, distributor, etc., in square brackets, even if the device includes the publisher's, distributor's, etc., initials or spelled-out name. Make notes as necessary about the basis for the identification, the source of the information used, the presence of the device, etc.

4C5. Fictitious or incorrect publisher, distributor, etc., statements

If the publisher, distributor, etc., statement is known to be fictitious or incorrect, supply a correction in square brackets and give the basis for the correction in a note. If, however, the entire statement consisting of place, publisher (distributor, etc.), and date is fictitious or incorrect, apply 4A4.

```
: Par Mathurin Marchant [i.e. John Wolfe]
Note: Printer identified in STC (2nd ed.)
```

4C6. Two or more names of publishers, distributors, etc.

4C6.1. If the publisher, distributor, etc., statement includes more than one publisher, distributor, etc., in a single source, transcribe all the names in the order in which they appear. Transcribe them as subsequent statements of publication, distribution, etc., only when they are not linked by connecting words or phrases.

```
: Par Ian de Tournes pour Antoine Vincent

: Printed for the author and sold by J. Roberts

: Printed for J. Newbery, T. Becket, T. Davies, W. Jackson, in
    Oxford, and A. Kincaid, and Company, in Edinburgh

: Ex officina Ascensiana : Impendio Joannis Parui
```

4C6.2. *Optionally*, if it is considered that the names are too numerous to list exhaustively, and that some may be omitted without significant loss of identification, the publisher, distributor, etc., statement may be shortened by omitting all the names after the third. In such cases, use the mark of omission and supply after it in square brackets a phrase in the language and script of the cataloging agency to convey the extent of the omission. Include the number of omitted publishers (or firms) and the number of omitted places (if more than one) in the supplied phrase.

```
: Printed for F.C. and J. Rivington, Otridge and Son, J. Nichols
    and Co. ... [and 26 others]

: Printed and sold by J. Newbery and C. Micklewright, also by
    Mess. Ware, Birt, Astley, Austen, Robinson, Dodsley, and
    Needham, in London ...[and 8 others in 8 other places]
```

4C6.3. If the name of a publisher, distributor, etc., associated with an earlier edition appears together with the name of the actual publisher, distributor, etc., of the edition being described, transcribe the names as a single element in the order in which they appear.

```
: Printed for T. Cooper, at the Globe in Pater-noster-Row, 1742,
    and reprinted for J. Wilkie, St. Paul's Church-yard
```

4C6.4. If both the place and publisher, distributor, etc., associated with an earlier edition appear together with the place and publisher, distributor, etc., of the edition being described, transcribe each publisher, distributor, etc., with the place to which it corresponds.

```
London : Printed by G. Riebau, no. 439, Strand ; Edinburgh :
    Reprinted, with permission, and sold by J. Robertson, no. 4,
    Horse-Wynd ...
```

4C7. Names of publishers, distributors, etc., in multipart monographs

If the publication is issued in more than one physical part and the name or form of name of the publisher, distributor, etc., changes in the course of publication, transcribe the publisher, distributor, etc., statement of the first or earliest part and give the publisher, distributor, etc., statement of the later part(s) in a note.

```
: G.J. Göschen'sche Verlagsbuchhandlung
Note: Vols. 8-10 have publisher statement: Verlag von G.J.
    Göschen
```

4C8. Supplied and conjectured names of publishers, distributors, etc.

If no name, address, or device of a publisher, distributor, etc., appears in the publication, supply the name of the publisher, distributor, etc., in square brackets if known. If the responsibility of a publisher, distributor, etc., for a particular publication is conjectured, either add a question mark to any supplied name or give the information in a note. In any case of a supplied publisher, distributor, etc., give supporting evidence in a note.

4C9. No supplied name of publisher, distributor, etc.

If no publisher, distributor, etc., statement can be supplied, use the abbreviation "s.n." (sine nomine) in square brackets.

```
Paris : [s.n.]

[S.l. : s.n.]
```

4C10. Publisher, distributor, etc., transcribed as part of another area

If no publisher, distributor, etc., statement appears in the publication, but the name of the publisher, distributor, etc., has already been transcribed as part of another area, supply it in a short identifiable form within square brackets.

```
[Paris : Symon Vostre, 25 Apr. 1500]
```
> (*Comment*: Title reads: "Ces presentes heures a lusaige de Paris ... fure[n]t
> acheuees lan mil cincq ce[n]s le xxv iour dapuril pour Symon Vostre, libraire ...")

If transcribing a publisher, distributor, etc., statement in the publication, distribution, etc., area, however, do not abridge or expand the statement simply because it repeats or omits information given elsewhere in the description.

4C11. Publisher, distributor, etc., statements in more than one language or script

4C11.1. If the name of the publisher, distributor, etc., appears in more than one language or script, transcribe the statement in the language or script of the title proper, or if this criterion does not apply, transcribe the statement that appears first. Transcribe the remaining statement(s) as parallel statements, preceding each by an equals sign. Make a note to indicate the original position on the source of any transposed statements.

4C11.2. *Optionally*, if it is considered that the parallel statements are too numerous to list exhaustively, and that some may be omitted without significant loss of identification, omit parallel statements after the first using the mark of omission. Transcribe the omitted statement(s) in a note, if considered important.

4D. Date of publication, distribution, etc.

4D1. General rule

4D1.1. Transcribe dates of publication, distribution, etc., as part of this element. Transcribe dates of printing or other manufacture only if appropriate according to the instructions in 4A6 (i.e., when the wording, layout, or typography of the publication suggests that the manufacturer is also functioning as the publisher, distributor, etc.).

4D1.2. Transcribe dates as they appear in the publication, including the day and month, if present.

```
, 7th July 1766
```

```
, 1732, reprinted 1734
```

4D1.3. Transcribe words and phrases such as "in the year" and "anno" as part of this element. If both the place and the date of printing appear in conjunction with the phrase "printed in the year," determine whether "printed" is to be transcribed with the place or the date according to the punctuation or typography of the source.

```
London printed : [s.n.], in the year 1742
```
    (*Comment*: Imprint reads: "London printed, in the year 1742")

```
London : [s.n.], printed in the year 1742
```
    (*Comment*: Imprint reads: "London, printed in the year 1742")

4D1.4. If the date is grammatically inseparable from information transcribed as part of another element or area according to one or more of the conditions enumerated in 1B1.1, transcribe it within that area or element and supply the date in square brackets as the date of publication, distribution, etc.

4D2. Transcription involving adjustments or additions

4D2.1. Roman numerals. If the date appears in roman numerals, transcribe the date as it appears. Omit internal spaces and punctuation (see 0G3.4, 0G4.1). Supply the year in arabic numerals in square brackets.

```
, anno Domini MDCXIV [1614]
```

```
, anno gratiae Mdiij [1503]
```

```
, MCCCCLXXXII le XV jour de decembre [1482]
```

```
, MDCCXLIV [1744]
```
    (*Comment*: On publication: "M. D. CC. XLIV")

4D2.2. Chronograms. If the date appears only in the form of a chronogram, substitute for it the date in arabic numerals in square brackets. If the supplied date includes a day/month, use the sequence: day, month, year. Make a note explaining the source of the date. Include a transcription of the original chronogram in the note, if considered important.

```
, [1740]
Note: Date of publication derived from chronogram: Ipso anno
   tertIo saeCVLarI typographIae DIVIno aVXILIo a gerManIs
   InVentae
```
    (*Comment*: Transcribing the chronogram in this note is optional)

```
, [8 Mar. 1643]
Note: Date of publication derived from chronogram in colophon
```

4D2.3. Very long dates. If the statement of the date in the publication is very long, substitute for it a formalized statement in square brackets. If the supplied date includes a day/month, use the sequence: day, month, year. Make a note concerning the source and the original form of the statement.

```
, [18 May 1507]
Note: Date expressed in Latin words on t.p.
      (Comment: In publication: "Anno gratiae millesimo quingentesimo septimo die
      vero decimoctavo Maij")
```

4D2.4. Fictitious or incorrect dates. If the year of publication, distribution, etc., is known to be fictitious or is incorrect, transcribe it as it appears and supply the real or correct year in square brackets. If, however, the entire statement consisting of place, publisher (distributor, etc.), and date is fictitious or incorrect, apply 4A4.

```
, DMLII [i.e. 1552]

, 1703 [i.e. 1730]
```

If a date from the title page has been transcribed as the publication, distribution, etc., date, and evidence for a later date of publication, distribution, etc., appears in a source other than the title page, supply the later date in square brackets as a correction. If necessary, make a note to clarify that the date added as a correction is a differing date of publication, not a correction of an error on the title page.

```
, 1786 [i.e. 1788]
Note: Dedication and preface both dated 1788
```

4D2.5. Julian/Old Style dates. If the year of publication, distribution, etc., is based on the Julian calendar (sometimes called the Old Style calendar) and the publication is known to have been published in the following year according to the Gregorian calendar, transcribe the date as it appears and supply the Gregorian year in square brackets.[15] Make a note to indicate the basis for the

---

[15] The Julian calendar was gradually abandoned in favor of the Gregorian calendar beginning in 1582, with different countries adopting the calendar in different years. The difficulty in determining dates during this period is further complicated by the fact that January 1 was not universally used to reckon the start of a new year (e.g., before adopting the Gregorian calendar, Great Britain and its colonies long calculated the turn of the year on March 25, the Feast of the Annunciation or "Lady Day"). For assistance in establishing Gregorian dates, consult a reference

supplied year. Do not amend the month and day, if present, by supplying Gregorian equivalents. In case of doubt, do not adjust the year.

```
, printed anno Domini 1640 [i.e. 1641]
Note: Date of publication based on the Julian calendar; see STC
    (2nd ed.)

, Februar. 8. anno 1588 [i.e. 1589]
Note: Imprint uses Lady Day dating; see Steele, R. Tudor and
    Stuart proclamations
```

If two dates appear in the publication, representing both Julian (Old Style) and Gregorian (New Style) dating, transcribe both dates, separated by a slash. Supply the Gregorian year in square brackets, if necessary.

```
, 2/13 September 1750

, 1690/1 [i.e. 1691]

, 1690/1691 [i.e. 1691]
```

4D2.6. Dates not of the Julian or Gregorian calendar. If the date of publication, distribution, etc., is based on a calendar other than the Julian or Gregorian calendar, transcribe the date and supply the equivalent Julian or Gregorian year(s) in square brackets.[16]

```
, shenat 627 [1866 or 1867]
        (Comment: Year follows Hebrew calendar)

, an VII [1798 or 1799]
        (Comment: Year follows French Revolutionary calendar)
```

Optionally, if the date of publication, distribution, etc., includes a day/month based on a calendar other than the Julian or Gregorian calendar, transcribe the date and supply the equivalent Julian or Gregorian day/month in square brackets. Use the sequence: day, month, year.

```
, prid. Kal. Dec. [30 Nov.] 1488
        (Comment: Day and month follow Roman-style calendar)
```

---

source such as Adriano Cappelli's *Cronologia e Calendario Perpetuo* or C.R. Cheney's *Handbook of Dates for Students of English History.*

[16] For publications issued before 1582, supply the equivalent Julian date(s). For later publications, supply the equivalent Gregorian date(s).

```
, die visitationis Beatae Virginis Mariae [2 July] 1497
```
        (*Comment*: Day and month follow ecclesiastical calendar)

4D2.7. Multiple adjustments or additions. If the date of publication, distribution, etc., requires more than a single adjustment or addition, provide all the supplied information within the same set of square brackets.

```
, MDCXIII [1613 i.e. 1693]
Note: Corrected imprint date from Wing

, anno MDCXVIII [1618 i.e. 1619]
Note: Imprint from colophon. Date of publication given in Old
   Style; see STC (2nd ed.)

, [620 i.e. 1859 or 1860]
Note: Date of publication derived from chronogram on t.p.
```

4D3. Date of publication, distribution, etc., supplied from reference sources

If the date of publication, distribution, etc., does not appear in the publication but is known, supply it in square brackets from any source, preferably a reliable bibliography or reference work. Give the source of the supplied date and any needed explanation in a note.

```
, [1876]
Note: Publication date from BAL
```

4D4. Conjectural date of publication, distribution, etc.

4D4.1. Supply in square brackets a conjectural date of publication, distribution, etc., based on any information available. Indicate the basis for the conjecture in a note.

4D4.2. If the title page bears a prominent date that does not clearly represent the date of publication, either transcribe it as part of the title and statement of responsibility area or give it in a note.

```
, [1814?]
Note: At head of title: December 25, 1814
```
        (*Comment*: Date at head of title is the date of the proclamation, not the date of publication)

4D5. Patterns for supplying a conjectural date

Give a probable date or period of publication, distribution, etc., according to one of the patterns shown in the examples below. Give any needed explanation in a note.

, [1560?]	probable date
, [ca. 1580]	approximate date
, [ca. 1580?]	probable approximate date
, [not before 1479]	terminal date
, [not after 21 Aug. 1492]	terminal date
, [1727 or 1728]	one year or the other
, [between 1711 and 1749]	span certain
, [between 1711 and 1749?]	span uncertain
, [167-]	decade certain
, [167-?]	probable decade
, [16--]	century certain
, [16--?]	probable century

4D6. Copyright dates and dates of deposit

4D6.1. Do not transcribe a copyright date or a date of deposit in the publication, distribution, etc., area.

4D6.2. If a date of publication, distribution, etc., does not appear in the source and it is likely that the date of copyright or deposit represents the date of publication, supply the date in square brackets as the date of publication. Include a question mark if the supplied date is conjectural. Make a note to indicate that the basis for the supplied date is the date of copyright or deposit. Include in the note as much information as is deemed important to the cataloging agency. If transcribing a copyright symbol in the note, use a lowercase **c** to represent the symbol if it cannot be reproduced using available typographic facilities.

```
, [1850?]
Note: Copyright statement dated 1850 on t.p. verso

, [1866?]
Note: "Entered, according to Act of Congress, in the year 1866
   ... in the clerk's office of the Dist. Court of the U.S., for
   the Southern District of New York"--T.p. verso

, [1976]
Note: Date of deposit in colophon: 1er trimestre 1976
```

```
, [1988]
Note: Page [4] of cover: c1988
```

4D6.3. If the date of copyright or deposit does not represent the probable date of publication, distribution, etc., note it nonetheless and supply a more accurate date of publication, distribution, etc., in square brackets. Provide an explanation for the supplied date if possible.

```
, [194-]
Note: Publication date suggested by WWII imagery on cover;
    copyright date of 1929 in colophon
```

4D6.4. If the publication bears both a date of publication, distribution, etc., and a date of copyright or deposit, the latter information may be given in a note, if considered important.

```
, 1880
Optional note: "Copyright, 1878, by F.B. Greene"--T.p. verso
```

4D7. Date of publication, distribution, etc., in multipart monographs

4D7.1. In describing a publication consisting of volumes, parts, or fascicles published over a number of years, transcribe the date of the volume, part, or fascicle published first and the date of the volume, part, or fascicle published last, and connect them with a hyphen.

```
, 1692-1702

, MDXIII-MDXXIIII [1513-1524]

, MDLVIII-1570 [1558-1570]
```

4D7.2. Record the date of each volume in a note, if considered important. Such a note is particularly useful when the order of publication, distribution, etc., does not correspond to the order of the volume numeration.

```
, 1560-1564
Optional note: Vol. 1: 1561; v. 2: 1564; v. 3: 1562; v. 4: 1560
```

4D8. Date of publication, distribution, etc., on part pages

If parts of a publication have individual title pages bearing dates that differ from the date pertaining to the whole publication, give these additional dates in a note. If, however, one of these dates is a more accurate reflection of the actual date of publication, distribution, etc., than the date pertaining to the whole publication, give it as a correction as instructed in 4D2.4.

4E. Place of manufacture

4E1. General rule

Transcribe names of places associated with printers and other manufacturers as part of this element when appropriate according to the instructions in 4A6.

```
London and New York : Frederick Warne & Co., [1878?] (London and
    Edinburgh : Printed by Ballantyne, Hanson and Co.)
```

4E2. Supplied place of manufacture

If the place of manufacture does not appear, or is transcribed as part of another area or element, supply the place of manufacture in square brackets. Use a modern English form of the name, if there is one, and include the name of the larger jurisdiction if considered necessary for identification. Provide a justification for the supplied place in a note if necessary.

```
New Haven, Ct. : Published by E.L. & J.W. Barber, 1840 ([New
    Haven] : Hitchcock & Stafford, printers)

London : Collins ..., MCMXLVII [1947] ([Northampton, England] :
    Printed in Great Britain by Clarke & Sherwell Ltd, Northampton,
    on Mellotex book paper made by Tullis Russell & Co. Ltd,
    Markinch, Scotland)
```

4F. Name of manufacturer

Transcribe the names of printers and other manufacturers as part of this element when appropriate according to the instructions in 4A6.

```
New York : G.P. Putnam's Sons ; London : John Murray, 1901
    (London : Printed by William Clowes and Sons, Limited ...)

New York : Oakley & Mason ..., 1868 ([New York] : Davies & Kent,
    electrotypers and stereotypers ... : Press of the New York
    Printing Company ...)
```

4G. Date of manufacture

Transcribe a date of impression or other manufacture as part of this element only if it has not been treated as the date of publication, distribution, etc., following the instructions in 4A6, and only if it applies, or is likely to apply, to all copies of the edition or issue being cataloged. Such situations will occur only rarely. Dates of impression or other manufacture associated with a substantially unchanged impression of an edition or issue may be transcribed in a local note, if considered important.

```
, 1989
Optional local note: Library's copy: "1990 printing"--T.p. verso
```

Alternative rule: If a decision has been made to create a separate bibliographic description for an individual impression, state, binding variant, or copy within a single edition or issue (see introductory section X.1.4 and Appendix E), transcribe a date of impression or other manufacture associated with a substantially unchanged impression as part of the date of manufacture element. Transcribe the date as it appears, together with any associated words or phrases.

```
, 1989 (1990 printing)
Note: Date of impression from t.p. verso
```

If the date of manufacture appears in the source without an accompanying word or phrase, supply one in square brackets as appropriate.

```
, 1956 (1959 [impression])
```

If the date of impression is known from a source outside the publication, supply it in square brackets.

```
, 1923 ([1924 impression])
```

If the actual date of impression is known to differ from the date of impression given inside the publication, supply it as a correction within square brackets.

```
, 1923 (1924 [i.e. 1925] printing)
```

In the above cases, give the source of the date of impression, if other than the title page, and any explanations in a note.

5. PHYSICAL DESCRIPTION AREA

Contents:
5A. Preliminary rule
5B. Extent
5C. Illustration
5D. Size and format
5E. Accompanying material

5A. Preliminary rule

5A1. Prescribed punctuation

For instructions on the use of spaces before and after prescribed punctuation, see 0E.

Precede this area by a period-space-dash-space *or* start a new paragraph.

Precede an illustration statement by a colon.

Precede the size by a semicolon.

Enclose a statement of format in parentheses.

Precede a statement of accompanying material by a plus sign.

Enclose physical details of accompanying material in parentheses.

5A2. Sources of information

Take information for this area from the publication itself.

5B. Extent

5B1-5B14. PUBLICATIONS IN ONE PHYSICAL UNIT

5B1. General rule

5B1.1. The statement of extent should account for every leaf in the volume as issued by the publisher, including leaves of text, leaves of plates, and blank leaves. It should not include leaves added as part of the binding or the binding itself.

5B1.2. Record the complete number of leaves, pages, or columns in accordance with the terminology suggested by the volume (or other physical unit) itself. Describe a volume with leaves numbered on both sides, or with leaves unnumbered and printed on both sides, in terms of pages. Describe a volume with leaves numbered on one side only, or with leaves unnumbered and printed on one side only, in terms of leaves. If the leaves of a volume are numbered and printed on one side only, state this fact in a note. Describe in terms of columns a volume so numbered when it is printed with more than one column to the page. If a publication contains sequences in more than one kind of numbering, record each sequence in its appropriate term as pages, leaves, or columns.

5B1.3. Recording the "complete number" as stated above means recording the number on the last numbered page or leaf of each numbered sequence as the basic statement of extent, with any necessary additions according to succeeding rules, e.g., 5B3, for the addition of unnumbered pages or leaves. Record arabic and roman numerals as they appear in the publication. Record roman numerals uppercase or lowercase as they appear. If the pages or leaves are lettered rather than numbered, record the first and last letters followed by the word or abbreviation indicating pages or leaves. Use arabic numerals to designate pages, etc., that are numbered in words or in characters other than arabic or roman and make an explanatory note.

```
x, 32 p., 86 leaves

lxiij, [1] p.

XII, 120 leaves

381 columns

a-h p.

99, [1] p.
Note: Pages numbered in words "one" to "ninety-nine"
```

5B1.4. If the leaves are all or chiefly non-letterpress, record them as leaves or pages of text rather than as leaves or pages of plates as in 5B9. Make a note to indicate that the leaves are non-letterpress.

```
LXXVI leaves
Note: Wholly engraved
```

```
[1], 13 leaves
Note: Engraved, with a letterpress t.p.
```

5B2. Normally imposed single sheets

For a normally imposed single-folded (i.e., 4-page) sheet, record the statement of extent in the same manner as for a volume. Apply this rule even if only one of the four pages is printed.

```
1, [3] p.
Note: Last three pages are blank
```

See 5B13-5B14 for all other single-sheet publications.

5B3. Unnumbered pages or leaves

5B3.1. If unnumbered pages or leaves (printed or blank) are not included in a sequence of pagination or foliation, count them according to the terms used to describe the rest of the publication or the part of the publication with which they are associated. In ambiguous cases count them as leaves when they are all printed on one side only; otherwise count them as pages. Use arabic numerals within square brackets. If the gatherings are discernible, include in the count blank leaves at the beginning of the first gathering or at the end of the final gathering when they are present in a copy in hand or known to be present in other copies. Do not count possibly blank leaves wanting according to signature count and not known to exist in other copies.

```
[8], 328 p.

[2], 328, [6] p.

iii, [1], 88 p.

64, [2] p., [3], 16 leaves

64 p., [2], 16 leaves
       (Comment: The unnumbered leaves introduce the following section)

64, [4] p., 16 leaves
       (Comment: The unnumbered pages are not closely associated with either adjacent
       section and one or more are printed on a verso)
```

5B3.2. Consider numbered sequences to include unnumbered pages or leaves falling logically within the sequence, counting back from the recorded number to 1.

```
[2], 40 p.
```
> (*Comment*: Pages are numbered 3-40 with four unnumbered pages at the beginning)

but `[2], 5-40 p.`
> (*Comment*: Pages are numbered 5-40 with two unnumbered pages at the beginning; there is no evidence that any leaves are missing)

5B3.3. Record in the following manner unnumbered blank pages or blank leaves interrupting a numbered sequence:

```
200, [8], 201-232 p.
```

5B4. Errata leaves

Include errata leaves (but not errata slips) in the extent statement whether or not they are conjugate with another leaf of the publication. Mention the presence of errata leaves and errata slips in a note (see 7B16.1).

```
136, [2] p.
Note: Errata on p. [137]
```

5B5. Advertisements

5B5.1. For pages containing only advertisements, include them in the statement of extent when they are clearly integral to the publication. This is the case when they:

> are included in the same pagination sequence as the text;

or   are printed on the pages of an initial or final gathering also containing leaves or pages of text;

or   are printed on a separate gathering in a publication that is continuously signed.

5B5.2. Make a note to indicate the presence of pages that only contain advertisements.

```
124 p.
Note: Advertisements on p. 119-124

121, [3] p.
Note: Advertisements on [3] p. at end

124, 8 p.
```

> *Note*: Advertisements on 8 p. at end
>> (*Comment*: Advertisements printed on the final gathering in a publication that is continuously signed)

5B5.3. Do not include in the statement of extent pages containing only advertisements that do not fall into any of these categories. Record them in a local note, if considered important (see 7B19.1). *Optionally*, make a separate description for the advertisements.

> 278 p.
> *Optional local note*: LC copy has publisher's catalog on an additional 8 p. at end
>> (*Comment*: Advertisements printed on a final unsigned gathering)

> 32 p.
> *Optional local note*: UCLA copy has an additional leaf at end, with advertisements on recto and the verso blank

5B6. Multiple sequences of numbering

5B6.1. If the style of numbering within a sequence changes (e.g., from roman to arabic numerals), record each differently numbered part of the sequence. If unnumbered pages appear between the two styles of numbering, record the total number of unnumbered pages in arabic numerals within square brackets.

> xii, 13-176 p.

> xii, [1], 14-176 p.

5B6.2. If the publication has duplicate sequences of paging, as is sometimes the case with publications having parallel texts, record both pagings and make an explanatory note.

> xii, [1], 35, 35, [1] p.
> *Note*: Opposite pages bear duplicate numbering

5B6.3. If a volume has groups of pages numbered in opposite directions, as is sometimes the case with publications having texts in two languages, record the pagings of the various sections in order, starting from the title page selected for cataloging.

> ix, [1], 155, [1], 126, x p.

5B6.4. If a volume has pagination of its own and also bears the pagination of a larger publication of which it is a part, record the paging of the individual volume in this area and the continuous paging in a note.

```
328 p.
Note: Pages also numbered 501-828
```

5B6.5. If the pages, leaves, or columns of a publication are numbered as part of a larger sequence (e.g., one volume of a multipart publication), or the copy appears to be an incomplete part of a whole, record the number of the first and the last numbered page, leaf, or column. (See also 5B12 for incompleteness at end.) Generally precede the numbers with the word or abbreviation indicating pages, leaves, or columns.

```
leaves 81-94

p. 713-797, [1]
```
       (*Comment*: Fragment, detached from larger work)

but `[2], 713-797, [1] p.`
       (*Comment*: A complete publication, such as an offprint, issued separately with this pagination)

5B6.6. If a publication contains more than three sequences of numbered or more than five sequences of numbered and unnumbered pages or leaves, preferably record all of the sequences. If it is not practical to record all the sequences (e.g., if they are exceedingly numerous), then employ one of the following methods:

a) Record the total number of pages or leaves followed by "in various pagings" or "in various foliations."

```
1024 p. in various pagings

256 leaves in various foliations
```

b) If one of the sequences is clearly the main sequence, record the main sequence and the total number of other pages or leaves.

```
416 p., 98 p. in various pagings
```

c) As a last resort, give one of the designations used for publications issued in more than one physical unit (see 5B15.1).

```
1 v. (various pagings)
```

If one of these methods is employed, record all of the sequences in a note, if considered important.

5B7. Expansions or corrections

5B7.1. Make a note giving more precise information about pagination or foliation, blank pages or leaves, or other aspects of collation, if considered important (see 7B10).

```
91, [1] leaves
Optional note: Last leaf blank

216 p.
Optional note: Pages [205]-[206] blank

vi, 744, [2] p.
Optional note: Leaves A7, B3, and C7 are cancels in some copies
Optional local note: LC copy: Leaves A7, B3, and C7 are
    uncancelled; the cancel leaves are between p. 742 and p. 743
```

5B7.2. If the number of the last numbered page, leaf, or column of a sequence does not indicate the correct number of pages, etc., either record the sequences exactly to indicate the source of the error or record the number as given in the publication and supply a correction in square brackets. Provide an explanatory note, if considered important.

```
xiv, 823 [i.e. 328] p.
Optional note: Page 328 wrongly numbered 823

232, 221-252 p.

or  252 [i.e. 264] p.
Optional note: Numbers 221-232 are repeated in pagination
        (Comment: Same numbering as in preceding example)
```

5B8. Lack of numbering

5B8.1. If the whole volume is unpaginated or unfoliated, count the pages or leaves and record the total in arabic numerals within square brackets. State the total in terms of pages or leaves, but not of both. Begin the count with the first page or leaf of the first gathering and end the count with the last page or leaf of the last gathering, as instructed in 5B3. Count all blank pages or leaves.

```
[104] p.

[88] leaves
```

5B8.2. *Optionally,* if determining the total number of pages or leaves of an unnumbered volume might damage an item in fragile condition, give one of the designations used for publications issued in more than one physical unit (see 5B15.1) followed by "unpaged" or "unfoliated."

```
1 v. (unpaged)
```

5B9. Leaves or pages of plates

5B9.1. Record the number of leaves or pages of plates at the end of the sequence(s) of pagination or foliation, whether the plates are found together or distributed throughout the publication. Record the number even when there is only one plate. Count a plate folded and bound at the inner margin as two leaves of plates. Count unnumbered leaves or pages of plates without regard for the terms used to describe the rest of the publication (accordingly, leaves of plates may follow sequences of pages and pages of plates may follow sequences of leaves).

```
246 p., 24 leaves of plates

246 p., [12] p. of plates
```
   (*Comment*: Plates are printed on rectos and versos of 6 leaves)

```
x, 32, 74 p., [1] leaf of plates

[12], 275, [1] p., [1], XII leaves of plates
```
   (*Comment*: All plates except the frontispiece are numbered consecutively)

```
246 p., 38 leaves of plates, 24 p. of plates
```

5B9.2. If a volume contains a mixture of unnumbered leaves and pages of plates, record the number either in terms of leaves or of pages.

5B9.3. Record folded leaves as leaves or pages of plates. Make a note to indicate any folded letterpress leaves, if considered important.

```
50, [2] p., [2] folded leaves of plates
Optional note: The folded leaves are letterpress tables
```

5B9.4. Count title pages (and added title pages) as leaves or pages of plates if they are entirely or chiefly non-letterpress (e.g., engraved or lithographed) and not integral to any letterpress gatherings. Make a note to indicate any title page counted as a plate.

```
64 p., [1] leaf of plates
Note: Plate has engraved t.p. on recto and blank verso
```

5B9.5. As a last resort, if a publication's gatherings cannot be ascertained, or it is otherwise difficult to tell whether a leaf constitutes a plate, record it in terms of pages or leaves of plates if unnumbered and pages or leaves of text if included in the pagination.

5B10. Folded leaves

Describe folded leaves as such.

```
122 folded leaves

230 p., 25 leaves of plates (some folded)

306 p., [12] leaves of plates (1 folded)
```

5B11. Double leaves

Count numbered double leaves (leaves with fold at either top or fore edge and bound at the inner margin) as pages or as leaves according to their numbering. Count unnumbered double leaves as pages (2 printed pages per double leaf) or as leaves (1 printed page per double leaf). Always indicate the presence of double leaves in a note.

```
[36] p.
Note: Printed on double leaves

[18] leaves
Note: Printed on 18 double leaves

72 p., 1 leaf of plates
Note: Plate printed on a double leaf
```

5B12. Incomplete publications

If a volume, or an individual sequence of pages or leaves within a volume, lacks pages or leaves at its end—or an unpaginated or unfoliated volume or sequence lacks any pages or leaves—and the paging or foliation of a complete copy cannot be ascertained, record the number of the last numbered or unnumbered page or leaf followed by "+ p." or "+ leaves." Make a note of the imperfection.

```
xxiv, 178+ p.
Note: Description based on incomplete copy; all after p. 178
   wanting

[8+], 237, [1] leaves
Note: Description based on incomplete copy; one or more prelim.
   leaves (incl. t.p.) wanting
```

5B13. Sheets, rolls, cases, portfolios, etc.

For a publication in a single physical unit other than a volume (e.g., a sheet, a roll, a case, or a portfolio), use an appropriate designation ("sheet," etc.) preceded by the arabic numeral 1. If adding a statement of pagination or foliation, place it in parentheses following the designation.

```
1 portfolio (26 sheets)

1 portfolio ([44] sheets)
```

5B14. Single-sheet publications

5B14.1. For a publication consisting of a single sheet designed to be used unfolded (whether issued folded or unfolded), add a statement of pagination based on the number of pages printed, not counting blanks, as follows:

```
1 sheet (2 p.)
```
    (*Comment*: Sheet of any size printed on both sides, numbered)

```
1 sheet ([2] p.)
```
    (*Comment*: Sheet of any size printed on both sides, unnumbered)

```
1 sheet ([3] p.)
```
    (*Comment*: Folded sheet with title and colophon printed as 2 pages on "outside;" all text printed as one page occupying the entire "inside")

```
1 sheet (1 p.)
```
    (*Comment*: Broadside or other sheet printed on one side, numbered)

```
1 sheet ([1] p.)
```
    (*Comment*: Broadside or other sheet printed on one side, unnumbered)

5B14.2. For a publication consisting of a single sheet folded into multiple panels, include in parentheses a count of the number of physical panels on one side of the sheet when unfolded. Include both blank panels and panels containing text or illustrations in the count. Enclose the number in square brackets. Provide details of the sheet's layout (including the numbering of the panels) in a note, if considered important.

```
1 folded sheet ([16] panels)
Optional note: A folded sheet with 16 panels on each side when
   unfolded. All panels are unnumbered.

1 folded sheet ([4] panels)
Optional note: A folded sheet with 4 panels on each side when
   unfolded. The "outside" contains a title panel, two panels
```

```
numbered 1-2, and a final blank panel. The "inside" contains a
large map spread over all four panels.
```

For a normally imposed single-folded (i.e., 4-page) sheet, see 5B2.

5B15-5B20. PUBLICATIONS IN MORE THAN ONE PHYSICAL UNIT

5B15. General rule

5B15.1. If a publication is issued in more than one physical unit, give the number of physical units in arabic numerals followed by the appropriate designation for the unit (see also 5E).

```
3 v.

2 portfolios

6 sheets
```

5B15.2. If a publication has been issued in fascicles intended to be bound into one or more physical units, give the number of pages, leaves, or volumes appropriate to its final form, with a note indicating that it was issued in fascicles.

5B15.3. If the number of physical units in which a publication is bound differs from the number in which it was actually issued, state this fact in a local note, if considered important (see 7B19.1).

```
6 v.
Optional local note: LC copy bound in 3 v.
```

5B16. Bibliographic volumes vs. physical volumes

If the number of bibliographic volumes differs from the number of physical volumes in which a publication is actually issued, give the number of bibliographic volumes followed by "in" and the number of physical volumes. Give details of the publication's numbering in a note, unless the numbering is given in a contents note (see 7B10).

```
3 v. in 5
Note: Vols. numbered 1, 2A, 2B, 2C, 3

8 v. in 5
Note: The t.p. of the 5th vol. bears the designation "Bde. 5-8"
```

5B17. Pagination continuous

5B17.1. If the pagination of a publication in more than one physical unit is continuous, give the pagination in parentheses after the number of units.

```
8 v. (894 p.)
```

5B17.2. Do not use the physical description area to record preliminary sequences unless only the first volume contains such a sequence. A complete record of sequences may be given in a note, if considered important.

```
3 v. (xx, 804 p.)
```
   (*Comment*: Preliminaries are in v. 1 only)

```
3 v. (804 p.)
Optional note: Vol. 1: xx, 202 p.; v. 2: xx, 203-512 p.; v. 3:
   xxi, [1], 513-804 p.
```
   (*Comment*: Preliminaries are present in all volumes)

5B18. Pagination not continuous

Optionally, if the pagination of a publication in more than one physical unit is not continuous, record the pagination of each unit either in parentheses after the number of units or in a note.

```
2 portfolios (12, 18 leaves)

5 v. (32, 36, 48, 36, 18 p.)

3 v. (v, [1], 31, [1]; vi, 32; iii, [1], 49, [1] p.)
```

```
or  3 v.
    Optional note: Vol. 1: v, [1], 31, [1] p.; v. 2: vi, 32 p.; v. 3:
       iii, [1], 49, [1] p.
```
   (*Comment*: Same pagination as in preceding example)

5B19. Leaves and pages of plates

If a publication in more than one physical unit contains leaves or pages of plates, do not record them in the statement of extent. Note the presence of the plates in a note, if considered important.

```
2 v.
Optional note: Vol. 1: viii, 100, [4] p., [12] leaves of plates
   (2 folded); v. 2: iv, 112 p., [9] leaves of plates
```

5B20. Discontinued publications

If a publication planned for more than one physical unit has been or appears to have been discontinued before completion, describe the incomplete set as appropriate (i.e., record paging for a single volume or the number of volumes for multiple volumes). Make an explanatory note.

```
2 v.
Note: No more published?

627, [1] p.
Note: Vol. 2 was never published
```

5C. Illustration

5C1. General rule

5C1.1. To indicate the presence of illustration, use the abbreviation "ill." after the statement of extent.

```
8 v. : ill.

492 p. : ill.

246 p., 32 p. of plates : ill.
```

5C1.2. *Optionally*, disregard minor illustrations.

5C1.3. Do not regard ornaments (e.g., head-pieces, vignettes, tail-pieces, printers' devices), pictorial covers, or pictorial dust jackets as illustrations. If considered important, these may be mentioned in a note (see 7B10).

5C1.4. *Optionally*, treat significant title-page illustrations as illustrations rather than ornaments. Make a note to indicate any title-page illustration so treated, if considered important (see 7B10).

5C1.5. *Optionally*, add the graphic process or technique in parentheses, preferably using a term found in a standard thesaurus.[17] Give more detailed descriptions of the illustrations in a note, if considered important.

---

[17] Thesauri useful for this purpose include the *Art & Architecture Thesaurus* (AAT) and the *Thesaurus for Graphic Materials II: Genre & Physical Characteristic Terms* (TGM II).

```
: ill. (woodcuts)

: ill. (steel engravings)
```

5C2. Types of illustrations

5C2.1. *Optionally*, specify particular types of illustrations. Use in alphabetical order one or more such terms as the following: coats of arms, diagrams, facsims., forms, geneal. tables, maps, music, plans, ports. (use for single or group portraits), samples.

5C2.2. Replace "ill." with terms specifying particular types of illustrations if the particular types are the only illustrations in the publication.

```
: maps

: ports. (Woodburytypes)
```

5C2.3. Precede terms specifying particular types of illustrations with "ill." if the particular types are not the only illustrations in the publication.

```
: ill., maps, plans

: ill. (wood engravings), maps (lithographs)
```

5C3. Color illustrations

5C3.1. Describe color illustrations as such using the abbreviation "col." Treat illustrations printed with a tint block (e.g., chiaroscuro woodcuts, tinted lithographs) as color illustrations.

```
: col. ill.

: ill., col. maps, ports. (some col.)

: ill. (some col.), maps, plans

: col. ill. (Baxter prints)
```

5C3.2. Do not describe hand-colored illustrations as "col." unless there is evidence that the publication was issued with the hand coloring. In case of doubt, consider any machine-press publication with hand coloring to have been issued that way by the publisher. Always mention publisher-issued hand coloring in a note (see 7B10.3); make a local note on the presence of other hand coloring, if considered important (see 7B19.1.3).

```
: col. ill.
Note: With hand-colored wood engravings
      (Comment: Title contains statement "with colored engravings")
```

```
: col. ill. (lithographs)
Note: Lithographs are hand colored, as issued; see Sitwell, S.
  Fine bird books, p. 78
```

5C3.3. If both the text and illustrations are printed in a single color, do not describe the illustrations as "col." Make a note to indicate the color of the ink, if considered important.

```
: ill.
Optional note: Printed in green throughout
```

5C4. Number of illustrations

Record the number of illustrations when their number can be ascertained readily (e.g., when the illustrations are listed and their numbers stated).

```
: 94 ill.
```

```
: ill., 8 facsims.
```

```
: 3 ill., 1 map
```

```
: 6 col. ill. (tinted lithographs)
```

```
: 2 maps (lithographs), 1 port. (mezzotint)
```

```
: 1 ill. (engraving)
Note: Illustration is a t.p. vignette depicting a woman with
  raised sword and torch, with two serpents rising out of an
  inferno in the background
```

5C5. Publications consisting entirely or chiefly of illustrations

If a publication consists entirely or chiefly of illustrations, account for this fact by specifying "all ill." or "chiefly ill." *Optionally*, when the illustrations are all or chiefly of a particular type (see 5C2.2), replace "ill." with the term specifying the particular type.

```
: all ill.
```

```
: chiefly maps
```

5D. Size and format

5D1. General rule

5D1.1. Give the height of a publication (based on the copy in hand) in centimeters, rounding a fraction of a centimeter up to the next full centimeter. If a publication measures less than 10 centimeters, give the height in millimeters. If more than one copy of the publication is held, and the heights of the different copies vary, record the height of the tallest copy and give the height of the other copies in a local note.

    ; 18 cm
        (*Comment*: A publication measuring 17.1 centimeters in height)

    ; 99 mm
        (*Comment*: A publication measuring between 98 and 99 millimeters in height)

5D1.2. If a publication is bound, measure the height of the binding. When the height of the publication differs by 3 centimeters or more from the height of the binding, specify both.

    ; 12 cm bound to 20 cm

5D1.3. For hand-press publications, add the bibliographical format of the publication in parentheses following the size statement whenever the format can be determined. *Optionally*, give the format also for machine-press publications. Give the format in abbreviated form (fol., 4to, 8vo, 12mo, etc.). Use "full-sheet" for publications made up of unfolded sheets.

    ; 20 cm (4to)
        (*Comment*: A publication in quarto)

    ; 20 cm (4to and 8vo)
        (*Comment*: A publication consisting of a mixture of quarto and octavo sheets)

    ; 51 x 38 cm (full-sheet)

5D2. Width

If the width of a volume is greater than the height, or less than half the height, give the height x width.

```
; 20 x 32 cm
```

```
; 20 x 8 cm
```

If one of the measurements would normally be given in millimeters and one in centimeters, give both measurements in millimeters.

```
; 95 x 120 mm
```

5D3. Differing sizes

If the volumes of a multipart set differ in size, give the smallest or smaller size and the largest or larger size, separated by a hyphen.

```
; 24-28 cm
```

5D4. Single-sheet publications

5D4.1. For a single-sheet publication issued unfolded, give the height x width. If a sheet is issued in folded form, but is designed to be used unfolded (e.g., with the chief part occupying a whole side of the sheet), add the dimensions of the sheet when folded.

```
1 sheet ([1] p.); 48 x 30 cm, folded to 24 x 15 cm
```

5D4.2. When describing other folded sheets (see 5B14), give the height of the sheet when folded.

```
1 folded sheet ([8] panels) ; 18 cm
```

5E. Accompanying material

5E1. General rule

5E1.1. If a publication and its accompanying material are issued simultaneously (or nearly so) and are intended to be used together, give the number of physical units of accompanying material in arabic numerals, and the name of the material at the end of the physical description.

```
; 24 cm (8vo) + 1 price list
```

5E1.2. *Optionally*, give the physical description of accompanying material in parentheses following its name.

```
; 21 cm (8vo) + 1 atlas (38 p., 19 leaves of plates : col. maps ;
  37 cm (fol.))

; 25 cm (8vo) + 1 map (col. ; 65 x 40 cm)
```

or   describe the accompanying material independently

or   mention it in a note (see 7B11).

5E2. Issued in pocket

If accompanying material is issued in a pocket attached to a publication, specify the location in a note.

```
; 30 cm (4to) + 2 folded maps
Note: Maps in pocket on inside back cover
```

6. SERIES AREA

Contents:
6A. Preliminary rule
6B. Title proper of series
6C. Parallel titles of series
6D. Other title information of series
6E. Statements of responsibility relating to series
6F. ISSN of series
6G. Numbering within series
6H. Subseries
6J. More than one series statement

6A. Preliminary rule

6A1. Prescribed punctuation

For instructions on the use of spaces before and after prescribed punctuation, see 0E.

Precede this area by a period-space-dash-space.

Enclose each series statement in parentheses.

Precede each parallel title by an equals sign.

Precede other title information by a colon.

Precede the first statement of responsibility by a diagonal slash.

Precede each subsequent statement of responsibility by a semicolon.

Precede the ISSN of a series or subseries by a comma.

Precede the numbering within a series or subseries by a semicolon.

Enclose a date following a numeric and/or alphabetic designation in parentheses.

Precede the title of a subseries, or the designation for a subseries, by a period.

Precede the title of a subseries following a designation for the subseries by a comma.

6A2. Sources of information

6A2.1. The prescribed sources of information for the series area are the series title page, monograph title page, cover,[18] dust jacket, and rest of the publication, in that order of preference. If the publication has both main series and subseries titles, however, prefer a source containing both titles.

6A2.2. If the series statement, or any of its elements, is taken from a source other than the series title page, make a note to indicate the source.

```
(The penny library of popular authors ; number 1)
```
Note: Series statement from t.p.

```
(E.D.E.N. Southworth series ; 35)
```
Note: Series statement from dust jacket

```
 (Britain in pictures : the British people in pictures / general
    editor, W.J. Turner)
```
Note: Series editor from verso of series t.p.

6A2.3. If the series statement appears on both the series title page and the monograph title page, indicate this in a note, if considered important, and record the text of the latter statement if the two differ.

```
(British poets)
```
Optional note: Series statement also appears at head of t.p.

```
(Blue and gold series ; no. 5)
```
Optional note: Series statement also appears on t.p. as: Blue & gold series. Num. 5

6A2.4. If the series statement appears as a stamp or on a label, transcribe it as found and make a note to indicate the presence of the stamp or label.

```
(New poetry series ; IV)
```
Note: Series statement from label on t.p.

---

[18] Consider the cover to be a prescribed source only if it was issued by the publisher. Series-like statements present on covers not issued by the publisher usually represent binders' titles and should be treated as copy-specific information. They may be transcribed in a local note, if considered important. In case of doubt, do not consider the cover to be a prescribed source of information.

6A2.5. If a series statement is not present in the publication, but reference sources provide evidence that the book was issued as part of a publisher's series, do not supply a series statement in the series area. Rather, provide the series information in a note, if considered important.

```
Optional note: Issued as no. 14 in the Brocade series. See
     Bishop, P.R.  Mosher, 148
```

6A3. Form and order of information

Transcribe series information in the form and order in which it is presented in the source, unless instructed otherwise by specific rules (see 0G).

6B. Title proper of series

6B1. Transcribe the title proper of the series as it appears in the publication, according to the general rules 0B-0G.

```
(The Edinburgh cabinet library)

(Harper's black & white series)
```

6B2. If the series title proper includes a statement of responsibility or numbering that is grammatically inseparable from other words in the title proper, transcribe it as part of the title proper.

```
(Tract no. I of the American Peace Society)
```

6C. Parallel titles of series

6C1. If the source bears a series title in more than one language or script, transcribe as the series title proper the title that is in the language or script of the title proper. If this criterion does not apply, transcribe the title that appears first in the source. Transcribe the remaining title(s), together with any associated information, as parallel series titles. Precede each parallel series title by an equals sign. Make a note to indicate the original position on the source of any transposed titles.

6C2. *Optionally*, if it is considered that the parallel series titles are too numerous to list exhaustively, and that some may be omitted without significant loss of identification, omit parallel series titles after the first using the mark of omission.

Transcribe the omitted title(s), together with any associated information, in a note, if considered important.

6D. Other title information of series

6D1. Transcribe other title information relating to the series, if present, following the series title proper.

```
(The mermaid series : the best plays of the old dramatists)
```

6D2. If there are parallel series titles (see 6C), transcribe the other title information after the series title to which it relates. If any parallel titles have been omitted from the transcription, also omit the associated other title information. Transcribe the omitted information in a note, if considered important.

6E. Statements of responsibility relating to series

6E1. Transcribe a statement of responsibility relating to the series, if present, following the series title. If the statement of responsibility does not appear in this position in the source, transpose as needed. Provide details of the transposition in a note. However, if the statement of responsibility is grammatically inseparable from the series title, see 6B2.

```
(Serie de libros de lectura / Mantilla)
Note: Series editor precedes series title at head of t.p.
```

6E2. Parallel statements of responsibility relating to series

6E2.1. If there are parallel series titles (see 6C) but the statement of responsibility relating to the series appears in only one language or script, transcribe the statement of responsibility after the last parallel title (following any other title information associated with the title).

6E2.2. If the statement of responsibility appears in more than one language or script, transcribe each statement after the series title (or other title information) to which it relates.

6E2.3. If any parallel series titles have been omitted from the transcription, also omit their associated statements of responsibility. Transcribe the omitted statement(s) in a note, if considered important.

6F. ISSN of series

Transcribe an International Standard Serial Number (ISSN) of a series if it appears in the publication.

```
(Graeco-Roman memoirs, ISSN 0306-9222 ; no. 62)
```

6G. Numbering within series

6G1. General rule

6G1.1. If series numbering is present, transcribe it as the last element in the series statement. If the numbering does not appear in this order in the source, transpose it as needed. Provide details of the transposition in a note. However, if the numbering is grammatically inseparable from the series title, see 6B2.

```
(Modern standard drama / edited by Epes Sargent ... ; no. XXXII)
Note: Series from t.p.; series numbering precedes series title
```

6G1.2. Transcribe the numbering as it appears in the publication. Do not use any abbreviations not present in the source and do not convert roman or spelled-out numerals to arabic.

```
(... ; num. II)
```

```
(... ; volume six)
```

6G2. If series numbering appears without a series title, transcribe the numbering in a note. Provide any additional information about the series (e.g., as found in reference sources) in a note, if considered important.

```
Note: Number "6" appears at head of t.p.; issued as part of the
   American tract series; see BAL
```
>   (*Comment*: Making a note on the number is required; providing the additional
>   information from BAL is optional)

In case of doubt as to whether a number appearing in the publication is series numbering, transcribe the numbering in a note.

6G3. Numbering relating to parallel series titles

6G3.1. If there are parallel series titles (see 6C) and the series numbering also appears in more than one language or script, transcribe each number after the series title to which it relates (following any other title information or any statement of responsibility associated with the title).

> (O.B.E.M.A ; number 11 = O.B.E.M.A. ; Nummer 11)

6G3.2. If the series numbering appears only once, transcribe it after the series title to which it relates. However, if the numbering relates to all, more than one, or none of the series titles, transcribe it at the end of the series statement.

> (Série bilingue = Bilingual series ; 5)

6G3.3. If any parallel series titles have been omitted from the transcription, also omit their associated numbers. Transcribe the omitted number(s) in a note, if considered important.

6H. Subseries

6H1. If both a main series and a subseries appear in the publication, give the details of the main series first, followed by the details of the subseries. If the main series and subseries do not appear in this position in the source, transpose them as needed and provide details of the transposition in a note.

> (Parlour library. Shilling series)

6H2. If a phrase such as "new series," "second series," etc., appears with an unnumbered series, transcribe the phrase as a subseries title. If the phrase appears with a numbered series, transcribe the phrase as part of the numbering of the series.

> (Studies in verse. Second series)
>> (*Comment*: Series is unnumbered)
>
> (Killaly chapbooks ; 2nd series, no. 6)
>> (*Comment*: Series is numbered)

6H3. If there are parallel series titles (see 6C), transcribe each subseries after the series title to which it relates. If any parallel titles have been omitted from the transcription, also omit their associated subseries. Transcribe the omitted subseries in a note, if considered important.

6J. More than one series statement

The information relating to a single series, or series and subseries, constitutes one series statement. If two or more series statements appear in a publication, transcribe each statement separately.

```
(American poets profile series ; 1) (Thunder City Press poetry
    series ; number 19)
```

7. Note Area

Contents:
7A. Preliminary rule
7B. Notes

7A. Preliminary rule

7A1. General instructions

7A1.1. Notes qualify and amplify the formal description, especially when the rules for such description do not allow certain information to be included in the other areas. Notes can therefore deal with any aspect of the publication.

7A1.2. Notes, by their nature, cannot be enumerated exhaustively, but can be categorized in terms of the areas of description to which they pertain. In addition to notes relating to these areas, there are notes that do not correspond to any area of the formalized areas of description. Occasionally it may be useful to group together notes which refer to more than one area, for instance when they are all based on one source within the work, such as a privilege statement.

7A1.3. If the description in the areas preceding the note area does not clearly identify the resource being cataloged, make whatever notes are necessary for unambiguous identification. When appropriate, refer to detailed descriptions in standard catalogs or bibliographies. Provide sufficient information to identify the specific source, whether using a general note, a formal "References" note giving the source in prescribed form (see 7B14), or some combination of the two.

7A1.4. Notes may also be made to justify added entries intended for special files of personal or corporate names, titles, genres/forms, physical characteristics, provenance, etc. Whenever possible, use terms taken from lists of controlled vocabularies when making such notes and added entries. Prefer the terminology used in lists issued by the RBMS Bibliographic Standards Committee.[19] Terms

---

[19] These lists include: *Binding Terms*; *Genre Terms*; *Paper Terms*; *Printing and Publishing Evidence*; *Provenance Evidence*; *Type Evidence;* and "Relator Terms for Rare Book, Manuscript, and Special Collections Cataloguing."

from other authorized thesauri (e.g., the *Art and Architecture Thesaurus*) may also be used as appropriate.

7A1.5. In general, notes are not required, but some notes are required in particular situations and are so indicated in previous rules, e.g., 1E3, 2A2, or 4A4, and in some of the rules for this area.[20]

7A2. Punctuation

Start a new paragraph for each note. End each paragraph with a period or other mark of final punctuation.

Separate introductory wording from the main content of a note by a colon followed but not preceded by a space.

7A3. Sources of information

Take information recorded in notes from any suitable source. Square brackets are required only for interpolations within quoted material.

7A4. Form of notes

7A4.1. Order of information. If information in a note corresponds to information found in the title and statement of responsibility, edition, publication, distribution, etc., physical description, or series areas, usually give the elements of information in the order in which they appear in those areas. In such cases, use prescribed punctuation, except substitute a period for a period-space-dash-space.

```
Revision of: 3rd ed. London : Macmillan, 1953
```

7A4.2. Quotations. Record quotations from the publication or from other sources in quotation marks. Follow the quotation by an indication of its source, unless that source is the title page. Do not use prescribed punctuation within quotations.

```
"Extracted from the minutes of the Society for the Propagation of
   the Gospel in Foreign Parts"

"Generally considered to be by William Langland"--Harvey, P.
   Oxford companion to Engl. lit.
```

---

[20] A complete list of required notes may be found in the Index under "Required notes."

```
"The principal additional music, contained in 72 pages, may be
    had, half bound, with or without the rules, price four
    shillings and ninepence"--Pref.
```

7A4.3. Formal notes. Use formal notes employing an invariable introductory word or phrase or a standard verbal formula when uniformity of presentation assists in the recognition of the type of information being presented or when their use provides economy of space without loss of clarity.

7A4.4. Informal notes. When making informal notes, use statements that present the information as briefly as clarity, understandability, and good grammar permit.

7A5. Notes citing other editions and works

7A5.1. Other editions. In citing another edition of the same work, give enough information to identify the edition cited.

```
Revision of: 2nd ed., 1869
```

7A5.2. Other works and other manifestations of the same work. In citing other works and other manifestations of the same work (other than different editions with the same title), give whatever information is appropriate, such as the main entry heading, title proper (or uniform title), statement of responsibility, edition statement, or date of publication. Arrange the information provided in the form that makes most sense in the particular case. Abridge the information as needed without using the mark of omission.

```
     Adaptation of: Bunyan, John. Pilgrim's progress

or   Adaptation of: Pilgrim's progress / by John Bunyan
```

7B. Notes

Some of the most common types of notes are listed below; other notes than those provided for may be made, if considered important. Specific applications of many of these notes are provided in the preceding sections. Make notes as called for in the following subrules, and, generally, in the order in which they are listed here. If a particular note is of primary importance, it may be given first, regardless of its order in this list. When appropriate, combine two or more notes to make one note.

7B1. Nature, scope, or artistic form

Make notes on the nature, scope, or artistic form when useful to amplify or explain the title proper and other title information.

```
An advertisement

A satire against William Pulteney

Prospectus for: Pope, Alexander. Essay on criticism. London, 1745
```

7B2. Language and script of publication; translation or adaptation

7B2.1. Make notes on the language and script of the publication, or on the fact that it is a translation or adaptation, unless this is apparent from the rest of the description.

```
Parallel Iroquois and English texts

English text with Latin and French prose translations

Text in romanized Arabic

Author's adaptation of his Latin text

Translation of: Gulliver's travels

In part a translation of: Le déserteur / M.-J. Sedaine

Adaptation of: Breviarium monasticum
```

7B2.2. Always note the presence of nonroman script in the publication if it has been transcribed only in romanized form in the description (see 0F2.1).

```
Church Slavic in Cyrillic script

Title in Greek script
```

7B3. Source of description; source of title proper

7B3.1. Always make a note on the source of the title proper if it is from a substitute for the title page.

```
Caption title

Title from colophon

Title from incipit on leaf [2]a
```

```
Title and imprint from printed wrapper
```

7B3.2. For multipart monographs, if the description is not based on the first part, identify the part used as the basis of the description.

```
Description based on: v. 2, published in 2001
```

7B4. Variations in title

7B4.1. Make notes on titles borne by the publication other than the one chosen as the title proper. If nonroman text has been transcribed in the title proper without parallel romanization (e.g., as transcribed from the source or provided by 0F2.2), give a romanization of the title proper.

```
Title on added t.p.: La naturaleza descubierta en su modo de
   ensenar las lenguas a los hombres

Spine title: Bath Road acts

Engraved t.p. reads: The continental tourist
```

7B4.2. If considered important, also include here partial or complete transcriptions of title information to show the actual wording of the title page (e.g., when information has been omitted) and explanations of cataloger-supplied letters or words (e.g., when special marks of contraction have been used by the printer in continuance of the manuscript tradition).

```
Marks of contraction in title have been expanded
```

7B5. Parallel titles and other title information

Make notes on parallel titles appearing in the publication but not on the title page; also give other title information appearing in the publication but not on the title page if it is considered important. If parallel titles and other title information appearing on the title page have been omitted from the title and statement of responsibility area (e.g., because they could not be fitted into the body of the entry, or because they were very lengthy), they may be given here as notes.

```
Title on added t.p.: The book of exposition = Liber rubens

Subtitle: The medicinal, culinary, cosmetic, and economic
   properties, cultivation, and folklore of herbs, grasses, fungi,
   shrubs, and trees, with all their modern scientific uses
```

7B6. Statements of responsibility

7B6.1. Statement of responsibility in source other than title page. If a statement of responsibility appears in a source other than on the title page, give it and its source in a note.

```
Dedication signed: Increase Mather

Signed at end: A lover of truth
```

7B6.2. Transposed statements of responsibility. Note the original position on the title page of statements of responsibility that have been transposed to the title and statement of responsibility area.

```
On t.p., editor's name precedes title
```

7B6.3. Attributions

7B6.3.1. If a statement of responsibility for a person or corporate body connected with the work does not appear in the publication, and an attribution is available, give the information in a note. Include the authority for the attribution whenever possible.

```
Attributed to Jonathan Swift. See Teerink, H.  Swift (2nd ed.),
    598

Published anonymously. By Stephen Jerome. Editor's dedication
    signed "R.H.," i.e., Robert Hobson, to whom the whole is
    sometimes erroneously attributed. Also erroneously attributed
    to Robert Harris and to Robert Henderson

Variously attributed to Dudley Fenner and to William Stoughton;
    sometimes also attributed to Henry Jacob
```

7B6.3.2. If a statement of responsibility recorded in the title and statement of responsibility area or in a note is known to be fictitious or incorrect, make a note stating the true or most generally accepted attribution. Give the authority for the information whenever possible.

```
By John Locke. Author's name appears on t.p. of 3rd and
    subsequent editions

"[Gregory King] was consulted about the coronation ... and was
    the principal author of the ... volume containing descriptions
    and splendid engravings of that ceremony ... though he allowed
    Francis Sandford to affix his name to the title-page"--Dict.
    nat. biog., v. 10, p. 131
```

```
"The identity of Junius, which he concealed with great skill, has
    never been definitely established ... He is now generally
    thought to have been Sir Philip Francis"--Oxford companion to
    Engl. lit. (6th ed.), p. 546
```
> (*Comment*: The pseudonym "Junius" appears on the title page)

7B6.3.3. False attributions appearing in the bibliographical literature or in library catalogs may also be noted, along with the authority for the false attribution and the authority for questioning it.

```
Attributed to Daniel Defoe (see Moore, J.R.  Defoe, 511);
    attribution challenged by: Secord, A.W.  Robert Dury's journal
    and other studies
```

7B6.4. Other statements. Record the names of persons or bodies connected with a work, or with previous editions of it, if they have not already been named in the description; give the authority for the information, if necessary.

```
At head of title: Sub Carolo. V. Romanorum maximo Imperatore,
    primo Hispaniarum Rege

Illustrations are woodcuts by Dora Carrington. See Kirkpatrick,
    B.J.  Virginia Woolf, A2a

Woodcuts on leaves B2b and C5b signed: b
```

7B6.5. Variant forms of names. Note variant forms of names of persons or bodies named in statements of responsibility if the variant forms clarify the names used in main or added entry headings.

```
By Gilbert Burnet, Bishop of Salisbury
```
> (*Comment*: Statement of responsibility reads: "by the Right Reverend Father in God, Gilbert Lord Bishop of Sarum")

```
Charles Pigott is the author of The virtues of nature
```
> (*Comment*: Statement of responsibility reads: "by the author of The virtues of nature")

7B7. Edition and bibliographic history

7B7.1. Note the source of any element of the edition area when it is taken from elsewhere than the title page. Note the original position of any element that is transposed to another position in transcription.

```
The statement "corrected printing" from colophon

The statement "amplified edition" precedes title on t.p.
```

```
Edition statement precedes author's name on t.p.
```

7B7.2. Make other notes relating to the edition being described or to the bibliographic history of the work, if they are considered important. In citing other works, and other manifestations of the same work, see 7A5. In citing bibliographies and catalogs, however, use the pattern for references to published descriptions shown in 7B14 whenever such a citation occurs in a formal "References" note.

```
Revision of: 2nd ed., 1753

Sequel to: Mémoires d'un médecin

A reissue of the 1756 ed., without the plates

Previous ed.: Norwich, Conn. : Trumbull, 1783

Detailed description of plates in: Abbey, J.R.  Travel, 23
```

7B7.3. If a statement as to a limited number of copies of the edition appears, give this statement of limitation in a note, preferably in quoted form.

```
"250 copies printed"--Pref.

"Limited edition of 20 copies"--T.p. verso
```

7B7.4. If the statement of limitation is accompanied by statements of responsibility or other information relating to the production of the edition, include as much of the additional information in the note as is considered important.

```
"350 copies of this book have been designed and printed by
    Sebastian Carter at the Rampant Lions Press ... hand-set in
    Hunt Roman, and ... Monotype Plantin Light with Monotype
    Albertus for the title. The paper is Zerkall mould-made wove.
    50 have been signed by Ronald Blythe, include an additional set
    of prints from the five blocks and are specially bound. Both
    bindings are by the Fine Bindery, Wellingborough"--Colophon
```

7B7.5. If the statement of limitation includes the unique number of the copy being cataloged, give only the statement of limitation here. Give the copy number in a separate local note, if considered important (see 7B19.1.3).

```
"Special edition of 200 copies on handmade paper"--Colophon

LC has no. 20, signed by author
```
(*Comment*: Given in a local note)

7B8. Publication

Make notes on publication details that are not included in the publication, distribution, etc., area if they are considered important. If elements of the publication, distribution, etc., area have been taken from a source other than the title page, make a note specifying the source.

```
Published in parts

Publication date from Evans

Imprint from colophon

Publisher named in privilege statement as Sulpice Sabon

Publisher statement on cancel slip. Original publisher statement
    reads: Sold by G. Walsh

Imprint judged to be false on the basis of printing of catchwords
    and signatures. See Sayce, R.A.  Compositorial practices (1979,
    reprint ed.), p. 3-6, 31

No more published

"Entered according to Act of Congress, in the year 1853, by O.K.
    Kingsbury"--T.p. verso

"Price three pence"

Publication date from outside back cover

At head of title: On the day of Lord Byron's death 1824

"Set by hand in Truesdell type by Arthur & Edna Rushmore at the
    Golden Hind Press, Madison, New Jersey. Printed on Rives hand-
    made paper from France"--Colophon
```

7B9. Signatures

7B9.1. General rule. Make a note giving details of the signatures of a volume, if considered important. Give these signature details according to the formula in Philip Gaskell's *A New Introduction to Bibliography* (see p. 328-332), insofar as typographical facilities permit. Preface this note with the word "Signatures" and a colon.

```
Signatures: [A]⁴ B-C⁴ D² E-G⁴ H²

Signatures: A-C⁴ D⁴(-D3) E-F⁴
```

```
Signatures: A-2Z⁸, ²A-M⁸

Signatures: [1-6⁸]
```
       (*Comment*: Volume is completely unsigned)

It is generally desirable to give signatures for incunabula, especially if identical signatures are not given in a standard bibliographic source. It is also desirable to provide signatures when a volume has no pagination or foliation.

7B9.2. Unavailable characters. If the gatherings are signed with a mark of contraction (see 0G8.2, Appendix G3) that cannot be reproduced using available typographical facilities, substitute the spelled out form and enclose it in square brackets.

```
Signatures: )(⁸ a-z⁸ &⁸ [con]⁸ [rum]⁸
```

If the gatherings are signed with other unavailable characters, substitute a descriptive term or an abbreviation for that term if a standard one exists.

```
[dagger]
```
       (*Comment*: Gathering is signed with †)

```
[double dagger]
```
       (*Comment*: Gathering is signed with ‡)

```
[fist]
```
       (*Comment*: Gathering is signed with ☞)

```
[fleuron]
```
       (*Comment*: Gathering is signed with ❧)

```
[maltese cross]
```
       (*Comment*: Gathering is signed with ✠)

```
[par.]
```
       (*Comment*: Gathering is signed with ¶)

```
[sec.]
```
       (*Comment*: Gathering is signed with §)

7B9.3. Special uses of *pi* and *chi*. Indicate unsigned leaves that fall outside the signature sequence (see Gaskell, p. 330) by using the words **pi** and **chi**. Do not enclose the words in square brackets. Do not use the Greek characters π and χ, as these will give the impression that the leaves have actually been signed with Greek letters (see 7B9.9).

```
Signatures: pi⁴ A–C⁴ chi² D–Z⁴
```

Indicate partial duplications of an alphabet (see Gaskell, p. 331) by using superscript **pi** and superscript **chi** or, if superscript letters are not available, by substituting "[superscript pi]" and "[superscript chi]."

```
Signatures: ᵖⁱA⁴ A–D⁴ ᶜʰⁱD⁴ E–F⁴
```

or   Signatures: [superscript pi]A⁴ A–D⁴ [superscript chi]D⁴ E–F⁴

7B9.4. Non-conventional Latin alphabet. If the gatherings are signed with roman letters according to a pattern other than the conventional 23-letter Latin alphabet (i.e., A-Z, less I or J, U or V, and W), make this explicit by recording the additional letters in the signature statement.

```
Signatures: A–V⁴ W⁴ X–Z⁴
```
>   (*Comment*: Indicates a 24-letter alphabet)

```
Signatures: A–I⁸ J⁸ K–U⁸ V⁸ W⁸ X–2I⁸ 2J⁸ 2K–2M⁸
```
>   (*Comment*: Indicates a 26-letter alphabet)

7B9.5. Signatures do not match gatherings. If it can be determined that the signing of the volume does not match its actual gatherings, indicate this in the note.

```
Signatures: [1]⁸ 2–3⁸; volume actually gathered in twelves
```

7B9.6. Concurrent signatures. If the volume is signed using two concurrent sequences, provide both sets of signatures in the note. Give the signatures that correspond to the actual gatherings first, if this can be determined.

```
Signatures: 1–12¹²; also signed A–S⁸
```

```
Signatures: 1–12¹² and A–S⁸; actual gatherings cannot be determined
```

7B9.7. Nonroman signatures (numeric sequence). If the gatherings are signed with nonroman characters that follow a numeric sequence, represent the characters using arabic numeration. Include an indication of the script used in the signatures in the note.

```
Signatures (in Hebrew characters): [1]⁴ 2–11⁴
```
>   (*Comment*: Indicates a numeric sequence in which the first gathering is unsigned,
>   followed by gatherings signed 2-11 in Hebrew numeration)

If the nonroman characters are accompanied by parallel numeration using another script, note this as well.

> Signatures (in parallel Hebrew and arabic numerals): pi^8 1-4^8
>> (*Comment*: Indicates a numeric sequence in which the first gathering is unsigned, followed by gatherings signed 1-4 in both Hebrew characters and arabic numerals)

In case of doubt as to whether a sequence is numeric or alphabetic, assume a numeric sequence.

> Signatures (in Hebrew characters): 2-3^8
>> (*Comment*: Indicates two gatherings signed with characters that could belong to either an alphabetic or numeric sequence)

7B9.8. Nonroman signatures (alphabetic sequence). If the gatherings are signed with nonroman characters that follow an alphabetic sequence, transcribe in original script if typographical facilities permit, or in romanized form using the *ALA-LC Romanization Tables*. Use uppercase or lowercase characters according to the usage of the piece. If the script is one that does not employ case, or if the case of the characters cannot be determined, use lowercase characters. Include an indication of the script used in the signatures if recording them in romanized form, or if the signature statement would otherwise be ambiguous.

7B9.9. Greek alphabetic signatures. For gatherings signed in Greek alphabetic sequences, use the 24-letter alphabet in the following chart as the basis for compressed signature statements (Greek letters are given in the top row, their romanized equivalents in the bottom row):

α	β	γ	δ	ε	ζ	η	θ	ι	κ	λ	μ	ν	ξ	ο	π	ϱ	σ	τ	υ	φ	χ	ψ	ω
a	b	g	d	e	z	ē	th	i	k	l	m	n	x	o	p	r	s	t	y	ph	ch	ps	ō

> Signatures: pi1 α-γ^2 A-2Λ^2
>
> *or* Signatures (in Greek characters): pi1 a-g^2 A-2L^2
>> (*Comment*: Indicates an alphabetic sequence with an initial unsigned leaf, three gatherings signed α-γ in lowercase, a full sequence of 24 gatherings signed uppercase A-Ω, finishing with a partial sequence signed AA-ΛΛ in uppercase)

7B9.10. Hebrew alphabetic signatures. For gatherings signed in Hebrew alphabetic sequences, use the 22-letter alphabet in the following chart as the basis for compressed signature statements (Hebrew letters are given in the top row, their romanized equivalents in the bottom row):

א	ב	ג	ד	ה	ו	ז	ח	ט	י	כ	ל	מ	נ	ס	ע	פ	צ	ק	ר	ש	ת
'	b	g	d	h	v	z	ḥ	ṭ	y	k	l	m	n	s	'	p	ts	ḳ	r	sh	t

```
        Signatures: א-שׁ⁸, a-k⁸
```

or
```
    Signatures: '-sh⁸(in Hebrew characters), a-k⁸
```
  (*Comment*: Indicates a Hebrew alphabetic sequence followed by a roman sequence)

7B9.11. Other nonroman alphabetic signatures. For all other nonroman alphabetic signature sequences, do not assume that a standard signing pattern can be used as the basis for compressed signature statements. Give the first and last characters in each sequence, followed by a total count of the gatherings in that sequence in square brackets.

```
    Signatures: A-V² [=41], 2A-2V² [=41], 3A-3Ω̄² [=24]
```

or
```
    Signatures (in Church Slavic characters): A-Ÿ² [=41], 2A-2Ÿ² [=41], 3A-3ŌT²
        [=24]
```

7B9.12. Full collation. If considered important, make a note giving the full collation instead of a note recording only the signatures.

```
    Collation: 8vo: A-H⁴; 32 leaves: p. [1-2] 3-62 [63-64];
        $3(-H3) signed. H4 blank
```

7B10. Physical description

7B10.1. Make notes on important physical details that are not already included in the physical description area, if considered important.

```
    The first and last leaves are blank

    Title and headings printed in red

    Volumes numbered: 1, 2A, 2B, 2C, 3

    Printed on vellum

    Printed on a quarter sheet
```

7B10.2. For incunabula, note color printing and record the number of columns (if more than one), the number of lines, and type measurements if no account is found in a bibliographical source and the printer is unidentified or has been identified from this information. Do the same for later publications, if considered important.

```
Printed in 2 columns; 38 lines; type 76/7
```

7B10.3. Give fuller details of the illustrations, if considered important. Always note the presence of hand coloring in publications issued as such.

```
Frontispiece on leaf A1

Woodcuts: ill., initials, publisher's and printer's devices

Engraved port. of author on t.p.

With hand-colored wood engravings, as issued
```

7B10.4. Describe details of an artist's book or a publisher-issued binding, if considered important.

```
Pictorial cloth binding with gold, brown, and green stamping on
   brown calico-textured cloth, designed by Margaret Armstrong;
   signed: M.A.

Toy book cut in the shape of a standing Robinson Crusoe

Collages of marbled paper squares and rectangles mounted on
   cream-colored Italian handmade paper (watermarked Umbria,
   Italy, C.M.F.)
```

7B10.5. Details of physical description given here usually apply to all copies of an edition or issue. Summaries of details that apply to particular groups of copies within an edition or issue may also be given. Notes pertaining to individual copies may be given separately as local notes, if considered important (see 7B19).

```
Two binding variants noted, one in red cloth and one in blue
   cloth

"The edition consists of 190 copies on Pescia paper and 10 copies
   on Japanese paper marked with the letters A to J"--Colophon
```

7B11. Accompanying material

Make notes for any accompanying material not recorded in the physical description area. Give the location of accompanying material if appropriate.

```
Accompanied by: "Star guide" (1 sheet ; 12 x 36 cm), previously
   published separately in 1744
```

7B12. Series

Note the source of any element of the series area when it is taken from elsewhere than the series title page. If any element has been transposed in the description, note its original position in the publication. Note any series information not transcribed in the series area, if considered important. Give information about a series in which the publication has been issued previously, if considered important.

```
Series statement from dust jacket

Series numbering precedes series title

Originally issued in series: Novelistas de nuestra época

Also issued without series statement
```

7B13. Dissertations

If the publication being described is a dissertation or thesis presented in partial fulfillment of the requirements for an academic degree, give the designation of the thesis (using the English word "thesis") followed if possible by a brief statement of the degree for which the author was a candidate (e.g., "M.A." or "Ph. D.," or, for theses to which such abbreviations do not apply, "doctoral" or "master's"), the name of the institution or faculty to which the thesis was presented, and the year in which the degree was granted.

```
Thesis--Harvard College, 1786

Thesis (doctoral)--Universität Tübingen, 1805
```

If the publication is a revision or abridgment of a thesis, state this.

```
Abstract of thesis--Yale College, 1795
```

If the publication lacks a formal thesis statement, a bibliographic history note may be made.

```
Originally presented as the author's thesis (Universität
    Heidelberg) under title: ...
```

7B14. References to published descriptions

7B14.1. Give references to published descriptions in bibliographies or other authoritative reference sources if these have been used to supply elements of the description. Use the form and punctuation conventions recommended by *Standard Citation Forms for Published Bibliographies and Catalogs Used in Rare Book Cataloging*. Begin the note with the word "References" and a colon.

```
References: Evans 24658
```
> (*Comment*: Made in conjunction with a general note reading: "Publication date from Evans")

7B14.2. Make other references to published descriptions, if considered important. Such references are especially useful whenever the cited source would serve to distinguish an edition (or variant) from similar editions (or variants), substantiate information provided by the cataloger, or provide a more detailed description of the publication being cataloged.

```
References: Gaskell, P.  Baskerville, 17

References: ESTC (CD-ROM, 2003 ed.) T60996

References: Lindsay & Neu.  French political pamphlets, 2194

References: BM STC Italian, 1465-1600, p. 368

References: Ritter, F.  Incun. alsaciens de la Bib. nat. de
   Strasbourg, 277

References: Palau y Dulcet (2. ed.) 19161
```

7B14.3. A general note may be made if a description of the publication being cataloged does not appear in a specific bibliographical reference source. Make such a note only if the publication fits the scope for that source and the source purports to be comprehensive for its scope. Preface the general note with the words "Not in" and a colon.

```
Not in: Martin & Walter.  Révolution française. Cf. IV:2, 9093
```

7B15. Summary

Give a brief summary of the content of the publication, if considered important.

7B16. Contents

7B16.1. List the contents of a publication, either selectively or fully, if it is considered necessary to show the presence of material not implied by the rest of the description, to stress components of particular importance, to provide the contents of a collection or of a multipart monograph, or to provide additional titles in a publication without a collective title. Note the presence of errata leaves and errata slips (see 5B4). Note the presence of errata listed in other sources in the publication, if considered important.

```
Includes bibliographical references (p. 43-58)

Includes bibliographical references

Includes index

"List of the author's unpublished poems": p. 151-158

Errata on last leaf

With an errata slip

Includes Joseph Pike's An epistle to the national meeting of
   Friends in Dublin
```

7B16.2. Transcribe contents from the title page if they are presented there formally and have not been transcribed as part of the title and statement of responsibility area. In such cases, follow the word "Contents" with a colon and the parenthetical phrase "(from t.p.)." If a formal statement of contents is not present on the title page, take contents from the head of the parts to which they refer, or, if this is not feasible, from any contents list, etc., that is present. For publications in two or more volumes, transcribe the volume or part designations as found.

```
Contents: (from t.p.) I. The good housewife's coat of arms -- II.
   The spinning-wheels glory -- III. The taylor disappointed of
   his bride -- IV. The changeable world

Contents: Love and peril / the Marquis of Lorne -- To be or not
   to be / Mrs. Alexander -- The melancholy hussar / Thomas Hardy
```

7B16.3. If a complete listing of contents cannot be assembled by one of the above means, the cataloger may devise a contents note from any appropriate source or combination of sources.

7B17. Numbers borne by the publication

Make notes of any numbers borne by the publication not transcribed in another area.

7B18. "With" notes

7B18.1. If the description corresponds to part of a publication that is made up of two or more separately titled parts that are also separately paginated or foliated and have separate signatures, but which have been issued together, make a note beginning "With" followed by a colon. List the other parts of the publication in the note, in the order in which they are found. In the case of bound volumes, list all the other parts on the record for the first part and, in general, only the first on the records for the subsequent parts. (Do not make such "With" notes when the pagination, foliation, or signatures of separately titled parts are continuous with the part being described. Instead, record these titles in a contents note as instructed in 7B16.)

7B18.2. For each work listed, give only the elements listed below:

   a) the heading; normally give this element first, usually in catalog-entry form (e.g., with inversion of personal names under surname, but not necessarily including personal birth/death dates, corporate qualifiers, etc.)

   b) the title proper as found in the record for the work; long titles may be shortened (whenever the uniform title is considered useful for the identification of the work, record it within square brackets preceding the title proper)

   c) the primary statement of responsibility as found in the title and statement of responsibility area of the record for the work, unless it is redundant of the heading or exceedingly lengthy

   d) the publication, distribution, etc., area as found in the record for the work, abridged as necessary, without using the mark of omission

```
With: Dunton, John. The merciful assizes, or, A panegyric on the
   late Lord Jeffreys hanging so many in the West. London :
   Printed for Eliz. Harris, 1701
```

7B18.3. If the works were bound together subsequent to publication, rather than issued together by the publisher, distributor, etc., make a local note according to the instructions in 7B19.3.4, if considered important.

7B19. Copy being described and library holdings (Local notes)

7B19.1. General rule

7B19.1.1. Make local notes on any special features or imperfections of the copy being described when they are considered important. Copy-specific information is highly desirable in the context of rare materials cataloging, which puts greater emphasis on materials as artifacts than is usual in general cataloging practice. Local notes can also provide warrant for added entries (e.g., added entries for the names of former owners or binders, for various kinds of provenance evidence, binding characteristics, etc.). Carefully distinguish local notes from other kinds of notes that record information valid for all copies of the bibliographic unit being cataloged.

For many older publications, however, it will not be readily ascertainable whether the characteristics of a single copy are in fact shared by other copies. In case of doubt, consider that the characteristics of the copy in hand are not shared by other copies.

7B19.1.2. The extent and depth of detail provided in local notes will be determined by the local policies of the cataloging agency. The rules set forth in this area are intended primarily to provide guidance and examples; the instructions are not to be seen as prescriptive.

7B19.1.3. Features that may be brought out here include known imperfections and anomalies, the presence of advertisements not recorded in area 5 (see 5B5), illumination, rubrication, and other hand coloring (unless issued that way by the publisher; see 7B10.5), provenance evidence (such as bookplates, stamps, autographs, and manuscript annotations), the names of persons or institutions associated with specific copies, copy-specific binding details and the names of binders, copy numbers (see 7B7.5), and "Bound with" notes.

7B19.1.4. Include in local notes one or more of the following identifiers, if considered important: a designation of the holding institution (e.g., a library's name, acronym, or code), a designation of the item's physical location (e.g., a shelfmark), or an indication of the item's copy number (if the institution holds more than one copy). Such identifiers are especially recommended if the bibliographic record is to be contributed to a union catalog or other shared database.

```
Copy 1: Imperfect: leaves 12 and 13 (b6 and c1) wanting; without
   the last blank leaf (S8)

Copy 2: Extra-illustrated

Folger copy on vellum; illustrations and part of borders hand
   colored; with illuminated initials; rubricated in red and blue

LC has no. 20, autographed by author
```

7B19.2. Provenance

Make a local note to describe details of an item's provenance, if considered important. In less detailed descriptions, it is advisable to summarize provenance information, without providing exact transcriptions or descriptions of the evidence. Include the names of former owners or other individuals of interest and approximate dates, whenever possible.

```
National Library of Scotland copy: inscription of John Morris,
   17th-century; stamped as a British Museum Sale Duplicate, 1787

Beinecke Library copy with inscription of Langston Hughes dated
   1954
```

More detailed descriptions of provenance might include such additional features as: exact transcriptions of autographs, inscriptions, bookplates, stamps, shelfmarks, etc.; location of each in the item; approximate dates when known; descriptions of bookplates using standardized terminology; descriptions of anonymous heraldic bookplates according to heraldic blazon; references to published descriptions of the collections of former owners of the item, particularly if the item is cited in the source, etc.

```
National Library of Scotland copy: "Ioh. Mauritius" (17th-century
   inscription on t.p.; see Birrell, T.A. Library of John Morris,
   no. 410); "Museum Britannicum" (ink stamp, in blue, ca. 1760,
   on t.p. verso); "British Museum Sale Duplicate 1787" (ink
   stamp, in red, on verso of t.p.)

Beinecke Library copy inscribed by Langston Hughes on t.p.:
   "Especially for Louise Bennett with admiration, Sincerely,
   Langston, New York, Oct. 8, 1954"
```

7B19.3. Bindings

7B19.3.1. Use local notes for descriptions of copy-specific bindings, if considered important; for descriptions of publisher-issued bindings common to all copies of an edition or issue, see 7B10.4-5.

7B19.3.2. Make a local note when the number of physical units in which a publication is bound differs from the number in which it was actually issued, if considered important (see 5B15.3).

```
Grolier Club's copy bound in 4 v.
```

7B19.3.3. Make a local note to indicate any errors in binding, if considered important.

```
Huntington copy: leaves I5-6 incorrectly bound between h3 and h4
```

7B19.3.4. Make a local note, if considered important, whenever a publication has been bound with one or more works subsequent to publication. Preface the note with the words "Bound with" followed by a colon. Formulate the remainder of the note according to the instructions in 7B18.

```
Special Collections copy bound with: The Bostonian Ebenezer.
   Boston : Printed by B. Green & J. Allen, for Samuel Phillips,
   1698 -- The cure of sorrow. Boston : Printed by B. Green, 1709
```

7B19.3.5. If it is considered that the works are too numerous to be listed exhaustively, make an informal note such as the following:

```
University of Pennsylvania copy: No. 3 of 7 works in a vol. with
   binder's title: Brownist tracts, 1599-1644
```

7B19.3.6. Make a local note to describe other details of a copy-specific binding, if considered important. Less detailed descriptions might include the color and nature of the covering material, a summary of any decoration present (e.g., "gold-tooled," "blind-tooled"), and (if these can be determined) an approximate date and the name of the binder.

```
British Library copy: late 17th-century binding in red goatskin,
   gold-tooled
```

7B19.3.7. More detailed descriptions of a binding might include such additional features as: nature of the boards (e.g., wood, paper); details of decoration; country or city of production; nature and decoration of spine; presence or former presence of ties, clasps, or other furniture; flaps; description of headbands, page-edge and end-paper decoration; references to published descriptions or reproductions of the binding (or related bindings), etc.

```
British Library copy: late 17th-century English binding; red
   goatskin, gold-tooled, over paper boards; gold-tooled spine
   with five raised bands; gilt edges; gold roll on edges of
   boards; marbled endpapers
```

8. STANDARD NUMBER AND TERMS OF AVAILABILITY AREA

Contents:
8A. Preliminary rule
8B. Standard number
8C. Terms of availability
8D. Qualification

8A. Preliminary rule

8A1. Prescribed punctuation

For instructions on the use of spaces before and after prescribed punctuation, see 0E.

Precede this area by a period-space-dash-space *or* start a new paragraph.

Precede each repetition of this area by a period-space-dash-space.

Precede terms of availability by a colon.

Enclose a qualification to the standard number or terms of availability in parentheses.

8A2. Sources of information

Take information included in this area from any source. Do not enclose any information in square brackets.

8B. Standard number

8B1. Give the International Standard Book Number (ISBN). Give such numbers with the agreed abbreviation and with the standard spacing or hyphenation.

```
ISBN 0-552-67587-3
```

8B2. *Optionally*, give more than one number, followed by a brief qualification as necessary. Give a number for a complete set before the number(s) for the part(s). Give numbers for parts in the order of the parts. Give a number for accompanying material last.

```
ISBN 0-379-00550-6 (set). -- ISBN 0-379-00551-4 (v. 1)
```

8B3. Fingerprints

If considered important, record the fingerprint derived according to a published standard in area 8 or in a note.[21]

```
165204-b1 A2 ade : b2 L we
```
> (*Comment*: Fingerprint constructed according to the rules for The Short-Title Catalogue, Netherlands)

8C. Terms of availability

Optionally, if the publication bears a price or other terms of availability, record the information in this area or give it in a note (see 7B8).

8D. Qualification

Optionally, add qualifications (including the type of binding) to the ISBN and/or terms of availability. Additionally, if volumes in a set have different ISBNs, follow each ISBN with the designation of the volume to which it applies.

---

[21] For further information on this method of identification and recommended forms of recording it, see *Fingerprints = Empreintes = Impronte*, supplemented by *Nouvelles des empreintes = Fingerprint Newsletter*, or Vriesema, P.C.A. "The STCN Fingerprint."

Appendix A. MARC 21 Descriptive Conventions Code

A1. Introduction

In MARC 21 bibliographic records, a code may be used in field 040, subfield ‡e, to indicate when specific cataloging conventions have been followed *in addition to* the conventions identified in the descriptive cataloging form (Leader/18). This appendix offers guidance in using "dcrmb," the code designating DCRM(B), in 040 subfield ‡e.

A2. Full-level DCRM(B)

Apply the code "dcrmb" to records for resources cataloged at full level (i.e., the normative application of these rules). The fact that such records follow the full-level provisions of DCRM(B) is indicated by the blank value assigned in the encoding level (Leader/17) and the code "dcrmb" in 040 subfield ‡e.

A3. Collection-level DCRM(B)

Do not apply the code "dcrmb" to records for resources cataloged according to the collection-level guidelines found in Appendix B. The fact that such records contain collection-level descriptions is indicated by the value **c** assigned in the bibliographic level (Leader/07). The guidelines in Appendix B suggest factors to consider in constructing collection-level records for rare materials and provide examples useful in a special collections context. However, the conventions conform substantially to those governing standard collection-level descriptions, as presented in *Cataloging Service Bulletin,* no. 78 (Fall 1997).

A4. Core-level DCRM(B)

Apply the code "dcrmb" to records for resources cataloged according to the core-level guidelines found in Appendix C. The fact that such records follow the core-level provisions of DCRM(B) is indicated by the value **4** assigned in the encoding level (Leader/17) and the code "dcrmb" in 040 subfield ‡e.

A5. Minimal-level DCRM(B)

Apply the code "dcrmb" to records for resources cataloged according to the minimal-level guidelines found in Appendix D. The fact that such records follow the minimal-level provisions of DCRM(B) is indicated by the value **7** assigned in the encoding level (Leader/17) and the code "dcrmb" in 040 subfield ‡e.

A6. Microforms and digital reproductions of books

Apply the code "dcrmb" to records for microforms and digital reproductions of books if the descriptive portion of the record conforms to DCRM(B) (full, core, or minimal level). If, however, DCRM(B) (full, core, or minimal level) is not used in all aspects (e.g., if the size of the book is not recorded in the physical description area), do not use the code "dcrmb."

A7. Nonbook formats

Do not apply the code "dcrmb" to records for nonbook materials such as serials, maps, music, and graphics, even though they may have been cataloged according to an adapted, "DCRM(B)-like" standard.[22] Do, however, apply the code "dcrmb" to individual and special issues of serials cataloged separately as monographs according to the provisions of Appendix H.

A8. "Special collections cataloging"

In this context "special collections cataloging" means fuller use of notes, access points, and other elements that are not specifically called for in AACR2 or its predecessors, but that follow the spirit of DCRM(B) without following its rules completely. Such cataloging is frequently done for 19th-century and later materials housed in special collections. Do not apply the code "dcrmb" to records for "special collections cataloging" unless the cataloging follows the descriptive requirements of DCRM(B) completely (full, core, or minimal level).

A9. Earlier codes

If an existing record contains an earlier code in 040 subfield ‡e, such as "dcrb" (*Descriptive Cataloging of Rare Books)* or "bdrb" (*Bibliographic Description of Rare Books)*, and the description is being updated to DCRM(B) standards, delete the earlier code and add the "dcrmb" code to the end of the 040 field in subfield ‡e.

---

[22] If one exists, use a DCRM component manual for the format being described.

APPENDIX B. COLLECTION-LEVEL RECORDS

B1. Introduction

B1.1. This appendix offers guidance in the creation of bibliographic records for collections of printed items that will receive collection-level treatment based on administrative or curatorial decisions. Several rationales can be cited to justify a decision to use collection-level cataloging:

› It can be a means of highlighting the shared characteristics of a collection of materials by providing a summary-level description, thereby "adding value" to any other forms of intellectual access, such as item-level records, and revealing collection strengths that may not otherwise be obvious.

› It can be a means of providing temporary control of unprocessed collections.

› It can be a cost-effective means of providing bibliographic control for low-priority items. Although this might seem to promise a solution to the problem of an institution's limited means, it should be understood that adequately arranging and processing collections prior to cataloging also takes time. Since there are significant costs associated with under-cataloged materials, this rationale should be used with careful consideration.

B1.2. A collection-level record may serve as the sole method of access for the collection, with contents information provided in notes. Some or all of the collection may also be represented by item-level bibliographic records, which may be created at any level of fullness using cataloging rules such as AACR2 or components of DCRM . Item-level access may also be provided for some or all of the collection through inventories, finding aids, or databases (referred to hereafter as "finding aids"), which may be linked to collection-level records. Providing some form of item-level access to resources represented by a collection-level record offers significant benefits for users and reduces the risk of redundant acquisition of those resources. Decisions about the appropriate type and level of description should be made based on institutional goals, priorities, and resources, as well as the attributes of the collections themselves.

B1.3. The following guidelines are based on those issued by the Library of Congress for collection-level cataloging published in *Cataloging Service Bulletin,* no. 78 (Fall 1997). Examples have been added, drawn from the types of collections likely to be found in rare books and special collections libraries. Catalogers creating collection-level records will also need to consult the appropriate cataloging rules, *MARC 21 Format for Bibliographic Data*, and their local system documentation in order to create useful, descriptive, and complete records using the various fields available to describe collections, as well as to create additional access points. Catalogers wishing to contribute collection-level records as part of the Program for Cooperative Cataloging will need to consult the relevant instructions in *BIBCO Core Record Standards*.

B1.4. These guidelines are *not* intended for description of traditional archival or manuscript collections. Rules for cataloging such collections are addressed in specialized sets of rules such as *Describing Archives*: *A Content Standard*. However, many of the activities associated with arranging and describing traditional archival or manuscript collections also pertain to collections of printed materials and inform these guidelines.

B2. Selection of materials

B2.1. Collections normally fall into one of three categories:

- groups of items that come to a library already well organized by a previous owner

- groups of items that come from a single source, but with minimal or no previous organization

- groups of items that are assembled into collections by the library for the purpose of processing and storage, and are therefore termed "intentionally assembled collections" (previously called "artificial collections")

B2.2. All three types of collections tend to be organized around one or more unifying factors, which may include:

- personal author

- issuing body

- genre/form

- subject

- language or nationality

- provenance

- time period

B2.3. Types of materials appropriate to consider for collection-level treatment include:

- groups of materials that share one or more of the above factors, and for which access can adequately be provided with a single classification number and/or a collective set of access points

- groups of pamphlets or ephemera in various formats that are judged not to merit item-level cataloging, but that collectively are of research value

B3. Arrangement and description

B3.1. Arrangement and description are terms used to describe various types of processing activities that bring order and control to collections of materials. They commonly involve the physical handling, sorting, and listing of materials, as well as preservation and housing activities. Additional guidance in these matters may be found in Kathleen Roe's *Arranging and Describing Archives and Manuscripts*.

B3.2. Arrangement. Arrangement is the process of sorting individual items into meaningful groups and placing those groups into useful relationships with each other. Materials can be arranged in many logical ways, and the design of the arrangement should be determined by examining the material to consider the types of access most likely to serve the needs of researchers and other potential users. Different collections will require differing levels and methods of arrangement. For these reasons, decisions about arrangement must be made individually for each collection.

B3.2.1. Organized prior to acquisition. For collections that come to the library already well organized, every effort should be made to maintain this order. Maintaining the original order of a collection can reveal significant information about the previous owner's use of the materials and is, for this reason, a basic tenet of archival practice.

B3.2.2. Organized by the library. Collections that come to the library lacking any recognizable order must be examined, sorted, and arranged in some fashion prior to cataloging. Collections consisting of many items are normally divided into hierarchical subgroupings. Customary types of arrangement include:

- by source or provenance

- by genre/form

- by content or topic

- in chronological order

- in alphabetical order (by author, title, etc.)

B3.2.3. Acquired individually. Materials originally acquired as individual items (whether simultaneously or over time) may be grouped in intentionally assembled collections, as noted above. Appropriate library staff, which may include curators and catalogers, must determine which materials will be so combined, how they will be arranged, and at what level of fullness they will be described (e.g., whether the material will receive contents notes and/or author-title analytics, whether it will be classified and shelved with book collections or boxed and treated archivally, etc.).

B3.3 Description. Description is the process of recording the information that was gathered during the sorting and arranging stages. For large collections, finding aids typically are compiled to provide a greater level of detail. Finding aids vary widely in format, style, and complexity. They generally consist of two parts. The first is a narrative introduction that includes: biographical sketches or historical contextual information; a content summary highlighting strengths, gaps, weaknesses, and characterizing the collection's extent and depth; and information concerning the collection's administration and use, such as restrictions on access. The second part is a listing of the items or groups of items that comprise the collection. For collections arranged hierarchically, the listings may stop at a collective subgroup level or may extend down to the file or item level.

B4. Elements of the bibliographic record

The rules that guide the bibliographic description and added entry portions of collection-level cataloging are the latest edition of AACR2, supplemented by use of appropriate national rule interpretations. Use the rules in conjunction with these guidelines, which are arranged by MARC 21 field. Fields for which no specific collection-level instructions are required are not included here but may be used as appropriate.

Leader and directory

> **06**: **Type of record**. If the collection contains only printed, microform, and/or electronic language material (e.g., books, broadsides, pamphlets,

serials, etc.), code as Language Material, type **a**. If the collection also includes other material types (e.g., cartographic, music, manuscript, etc.), code as Mixed Materials, type **p**.

07: **Bibliographic level**. Use the value **c** (collection-level).

Control field: 008

06: **Type of date.** Coding choices are: **i** (inclusive dates of collection), **k** (range of years of bulk of collection), and **m** (multiple dates).

07-10: **Date 1.** Give the earliest date, or single date, from the 260 field.

11-14: **Date 2.** Give the latest or closing date from the 260 field. Enter **9999** in 008/11-14 if the collection is open or not yet complete and use **m** in 008/06.

15: **Country of publication**. If all the items were published in a single country (or state, province, etc.), enter the code for that country. If the items were published in more than one country, enter the code **vp_**.

1XX field: Main entry

The main entry heading is determined by application of the appropriate cataloging rules. Title main entry is appropriate for many collections (see AACR2 rule 21.7). A 1XX name main entry is appropriate when all materials have the same personal author(s) or emanate from a single corporate body (AACR2 rule 21.4), including collections of laws with main entry under jurisdiction (AACR2 rule 21.31B1).

```
110  1   ‡a Austria.
```

When a collection is known by the name of its collector, enter the record under the heading for that person or body. *Optionally,* follow the heading by the relator term "collector" in subfield ‡e or the relator code "col" in subfield ‡4.[23]

```
100  1   ‡a Purland, Theodocius, ‡e collector.
245  10  ‡a [Theodocius Purland collection of materials on
             mesmerism].
```

---

[23] For more information, see the RBMS guidelines in "Relator Terms for Rare Book, Manuscript, and Special Collections Cataloguing."

240 field: **Uniform title**

Supply a uniform title for the collection if appropriate according to AACR2 chapter 25.

```
110  1   ‡a Austria.
240  10  ‡a Laws, etc. (Royal decrees)
```

245 field: **Title statement**

Construct a title for the collection and enclose it in square brackets. Devised titles should generally be in the language and script of the cataloging agency and should be both descriptive and distinctive, thereby highlighting the factor(s) that characterize the collection as a whole. Strive for consistency in title construction across collections. Types of data appropriate for inclusion in collective titles include:

› name of collection (for previously named collections)

› name of creator, creating body, collector or source (provenance)

› languages

› geographic locations

› genre/forms of material

› principal subjects—persons, events, topics, activities, objects, and dates of subject coverage

```
110  1   ‡a Austria.
240  10  ‡a Laws, etc. (Royal decrees)
245  10  ‡a [Collection of decrees of Emperor Francis I of
             Austria].

245  00  ‡a [Association of American Railroads collection of
             pamphlets].

245  00  ‡a [Analecta Anglicana : ‡b commonplace books].

245  00  ‡a [Spanish Civil War news releases].
```

246 field: **Variant form of title**

Record variant titles by which a collection may be known if they differ substantially from the 245 title statement and provide a useful access point. If most or all of the items in the collection have the same title information and it is considered important, make an added entry for the title.

```
245  10   ‡a [William J. Griffith collection on Central America].
246  3    ‡a Griffith Guatemala collection

245  10   ‡a [Collection of decrees of Emperor Francis I of
             Austria].
246  1    ‡i Decrees begin: ‡a Wir Franz der Erste, von Gottes
             Gnaden Kaiser von Oesterreich ...
```

260 field: Publication, distribution, etc. (Imprint)

All elements of the imprint may be included in collection-level records if appropriate. Bracket all elements that are used. In most cases, only the date element (subfield ‡c) is appropriate. Use 260 subfields ‡a, ‡b, ‡e, and ‡f only if the same place and/or the same publisher, printer, or bookseller apply to all items in the collection. If the collection is finite, use a single date or inclusive dates in the subfield ‡c, as appropriate.

```
260       ‡c [1780-1860, bulk 1795-1840]

260       ‡c [1655-1687]

260       ‡c [ca. 1500-ca. 1600]

260       ‡a [Madrid : ‡b El Partido Nacional, ‡c 1835-]

260       ‡a [Philadelphia, ‡c 1850-1890]
```

300 field: Physical description

Extent. Give the extent of the collection by counting or estimating the number of items it contains. *Optionally*, provide a separate physical description for each format.

```
300       ‡a 17 v.

300       ‡a 25 items

300       ‡a ca. 350 pieces

300       ‡a ca. 450 broadsides
```

Other physical details. Provide other details of particular significance.

Dimensions. *Optionally*, provide details of the size of the items and/or their containers. A range of sizes may be used if the items or containers are not of uniform size.

```
300       ‡a ... ; ‡c 28 cm.
```

```
300        ‡a ... ; ‡c 23-30 cm.

300        ‡a ... ; ‡c 60 x 90 cm or smaller.

300        ‡a 20 pamphlets ; ‡c in box 12 x 26 x 35 cm.
```

351 field: Organization and arrangement

Describe the way in which materials have been subdivided into smaller units or the order in which particular units have been arranged.

```
351        ‡a Organized in three series: 1. Poetry. 2. Fiction. 3.
             Essays.

351        ‡a Items are arranged chronologically.
```

4XX fields: Series statement

Do not use. If series titles of items in the collection are significant, trace them in the appropriate 7XX field. A note supporting the tracing may also be provided.

```
500        ‡a Most of the pamphlets are from the series Dicks'
             standard plays.
730  0     ‡a Dicks' standard plays.
```

5XX fields: Notes

Inclusion of a variety of notes will help provide collective context to the materials being described. It is particularly important to describe the contents of the collection in a 505 contents note and/or a 520 summary note, as described below. The order of notes presented below is recommended based on archival collection-level cataloging practice.

500 field: General note

Always include as the first note the statement "Collection title devised by cataloger."

506 field: Restrictions on access

When access to a collection or a portion thereof is restricted, explain the nature and extent of the restrictions.

```
506        ‡a Restricted: Original materials are extremely fragile;
             ‡c Researchers must use microfilm.
```

```
506        ‡3 All materials except pamphlets are restricted until
           Jan. 1, 2050.
```

545 field: Biographical or historical note

Provide biographical or historical information about the individual or organization referenced in the 1XX or 245 field.

```
545        ‡a Screenwriter for film and television, playwright and
           author.

545        ‡a George Heard Hamilton was born June 23, 1910, in
           Pittsburgh, Pennsylvania. He studied at Yale
           University where he received a B.A. in English in
           1932, an M.A. in History in 1934, and a Ph.D. in Art
           History in 1942 ...

110   2    ‡a Monday Evening Concerts of Los Angeles.
245   10   ‡a [Monday Evening Concerts programs].
545        ‡a The Monday Evening Concerts, first known as Evenings
           on the Roof, began in 1939 under the direction of
           Peter Yates. The concerts featured his wife Frances
           Mullen, among others, playing chamber music and other
           experimental works ...
```

520 field: Summary, etc.

Summary notes are narrative, free-text statements of the scope and contents of collections. Details may include forms of materials, dates of subject coverage, and the most significant topics, persons, places, or events. A summary note may be used in lieu of or in addition to a 505 note. If the collection contents are listed in a separate finding aid, use only a 520 note and also make a 555 finding aid note.

```
520        ‡a Pamphlets relating to the High Church's disciplinary
           hearings on Karl Sydow, held because of Sydow's
           position (both preached and published) on the
           interpretation of Christ's birth.
```

505 field: Formatted contents note

Formatted contents notes provide an ISBD-structured method of recording item-level information. Elements may include author, title, edition, date of creation or publication, extent, scale, etc. Assign a number to each item, record it within square brackets in the 505 note, and write it on each item. For materials that lack routine bibliographic indicia, or for large collections of many items, prefer the more narrative 520 summary note to the 505 note.

```
505  0    ‡a [1] Espagne rouge & noire [1963?] -- [2] The Spanish
          regime helps communism [1960?] -- [3] El marxismo en
          España / por Luis Araquistain [1957?] ...
```

524 field: Preferred citation

Use to provide a specific citation format for citing the collection.

```
524       ‡a Early Paperback Collection. Rare Books and
          Manuscripts Library, The Ohio State University.
```

541 field: Immediate source of acquisition

Record the immediate source from which the library acquired the collection. Use only for materials acquired as a collection.

```
541       ‡a Acquired by exchange from Auburn University; ‡d 1954.

541       ‡a Received: 5/22/1989; ‡3 master copy; ‡c gift; ‡a Mrs.
          James Hickey.

541       ‡a On permanent loan from the J. Paul Getty Museum.
```

555 field: Cumulative index/finding aids note

Specify the existence of any separate finding aid. An external electronic finding aid may be linked to from this field, if permitted by the local system (see also the 856 field).

```
555  8    ‡a Inventory available in the Wesleyan University
          Department of Special Collections and University
          Archives; ‡c item-level control.
```

561 field: Provenance note

Briefly describe any relevant history concerning the ownership of the materials from the time of their creation up until the time of their acquisition by the library.

```
561       ‡a The collection belonged to the Earls of Westmoreland
          from 1759-1942.
```

580 field: Linking entry complexity note

Use this note to state the relationship between the materials described and a broader collection of which it is a part. Use only when parts of the collection are being described in separate records (see also the 7XX fields).

```
580        ‡a Forms part of the Margaret Mead Collection.
773  1     ‡t Margaret Mead Collection
```

6XX fields: Subject headings

Assign subject headings as specific as the collection warrants.

```
245  00  ‡a [Janus Press miscellaneous printed ephemera].
610  20  ‡a Janus Press.
600  10  ‡a Van Vliet, Claire.
650   0  ‡a Artists' books ‡z Vermont ‡z West Burke.
650   0  ‡a Paper, Handmade ‡z Vermont ‡z West Burke.

245  00  ‡a [Italian Communist Party pamphlets].
610  20  ‡a Partito comunista italiano.
651   0  ‡a Italy ‡x Politics and government ‡y 20th century.
```

Assign as many subject headings as seem appropriate, remembering that economy in processing may suggest that a reasonable limit be observed.

655 fields: Genre/form headings

Assign as applicable. Prefer terms found in the official thesauri maintained by the RBMS Bibliographic Standards Committee;[24] terms from other authorized thesauri (e.g., the *Art and Architecture Thesaurus*) may also be used as appropriate. As with subject headings, assign headings as specifically and numerously as the collection and institutional policy warrant.

```
245  00  ‡a [American theater programs of the late 19th and 20th
             centuries].
655   7  ‡a Theater programs ‡z United States ‡y 19th century. ‡2
             rbgenr
655   7  ‡a Theater programs ‡z United States ‡y 20th century. ‡2
             rbgenr

100   1  ‡a Elliott, Harrison, ‡d 1879-1954, ‡e collector.
245  10  ‡a [Paper specimens and research material relating to
             the history of papermaking].
655   7  ‡a Handmade papers (Paper). ‡2 rbpap
655   7  ‡a Mould-made papers (Paper). ‡2 rbpap
```

---

[24] These thesauri include: *Binding Terms*; *Genre Terms*; *Paper Terms*; *Printing and Publishing Evidence*; *Provenance Evidence*; and *Type Evidence*.

7XX fields: **Added entries**

Types of added entries considered useful for various types of materials include: author/title analytics, government bodies or individual sovereigns (e.g., as authors of the laws, etc.), creators of collections, names of collections, etc. In cases where a person or corporate body is both the author or issuing body and the subject of a collection, it may be appropriate to provide both a 6XX subject entry and a 1XX or 7XX entry. If a linking entry complexity note has been used in field 580 to describe the relationship of the collection being cataloged to a larger collection, make an added entry for the larger collection using field 773.

856 field: **Electronic location and access**

Use to specify the location or means of access to an electronic finding aid prepared for the collection or for other reasons, such as to point to scanned items or digital images selected from the collection. Take special note of the second indicator, which specifies the relationship of the electronic resource being linked to the item described in the record.

```
856  42  ‡3 Finding aid ‡u
         http://lcweb2.loc.gov/ammem/ead/jackson.sgm
```

B5. Additional considerations

B5.1. Lengthy descriptions divided into more than one record. It may be desirable to divide the description of a collection into more than one bibliographic record due to factors such as complexity or length of the description or system limitations on record length. The description may be divided in whatever way is most sensible. For example, the collection may be organized in logical groupings, each of which can be represented in a single record (e.g., pamphlets concerning tobacco consumption, pamphlets encouraging smoking, and pamphlets discouraging smoking). Alternatively, a new record may be started at a logical breaking point, such as with every twentieth item, based on chronology, etc.

When multiple bibliographic records are created for one collection, most data elements will be the same across all records, according to the guidelines discussed above, with the following exceptions:

> *245 field*: *Title statement.* Indicate in subfield ‡n which part of the collection is being represented in the record.

260 field: *Publication, distribution, etc. (Imprint).* If the collection is divided based on chronology, include the appropriate range of dates in each record.

300 field: *Physical description.* Indicate in the extent statement in the subfield ‡a of each record the number of items represented in the record out of the total number of items in the collection, using terminology appropriate to the material being described.

```
300        ‡a Items 1-40 of 80 in 1 bound volume

300        ‡a Items 41-80 of 80 in 1 bound volume
```

5XX fields: *Notes.* With the exception of the 505 contents note (see below), give the same 5XX fields in each record. In addition, indicate in a note in each record that the collection being cataloged is represented by more than one record, and provide references to the other records.

505 field: *Contents note.* List in a 505 note only those items described in the particular record. Numbering within contents notes should be consecutive from one record to another.

B5.2. Considerations when adding to collections. Sometimes items are added to collections after initial processing or cataloging has been completed. In such cases, edit or add to the description as necessary, paying particular attention to the following elements:

- ‣ Dates (260 field and fixed fields)
- ‣ Extent (300 field)
- ‣ Contents (505 and/or 520 field)
- ‣ Subject and genre/form headings (6XX fields)
- ‣ Added entries (7XX fields)

APPENDIX C. CORE-LEVEL RECORDS

C1. Introduction

The elements of description provided in DCRM(B) constitute a full set of information for describing rare materials. This appendix sets out a less-than-full level of description containing those elements required by the Program for Cooperative Cataloging (PCC) in its standard for core-level records for rare materials. The core record standard was defined by the PCC for use within the context of its national cataloging program, BIBCO, to support the goal of providing cost-effective cataloging that meets commonly accepted standards.

Although the core record standard originated with the BIBCO program, it can be used by any library, BIBCO participant or not. Headings on all DCRM(B) core-level records contributed to BIBCO must be supported by authority records in the LC/NACO and LC/SACO Authority Files, with the exception of certain series headings. Authority records are not required for headings on other DCRM(B) core-level records.

C2. Application

Catalogers may apply the core-level standard to any rare materials described using DCRM(B), with one exception: it is not to be applied to books printed before 1501 (incunabula). DCRM(B) core-level records are especially appropriate when faithful and accurate descriptions are desirable, and the provision of subject and other access points is important, but abridged transcriptions and fewer notes are acceptable.

For rare books, the commitment, on the cataloger's part, is to render bibliographic details of the book as accurately as possible insofar as they are presented by the specimen in hand; also, to ensure that they are scrupulously stated, according to the provisions of DCRM(B). The strength of DCRM(B) is that it provides for "expanded coverage" of books deserving such treatment; conversely, it is possible to use those provisions for expansion as guidelines for trimming the description. By omitting most notes and taking the options given in DCRM(B) for abbreviating descriptive areas, or by not taking the options to expand the same areas, an effective DCRM(B) core-level record can be created.

C3. Elements of the bibliographic record

Use the guidelines set forth below, taken from the BIBCO Core Record Standards, to create core-level records using DCRM(B).

Leader and directory

Depending on the individual automated system or bibliographic utility, part or all of the leader and directory may be system-supplied. Generally speaking, the cataloger will have to supply values for the following leader positions:

06	Type of record
07	Bibliographic level
17	Encoding level
18	Descriptive cataloging form

Give the encoding level (Leader/17) a value of **4** to indicate a core-level record.

Control fields: 001, 003, 005

These fields are generally system-supplied.

Control field: 007

Code the following positions of the Microform 007 if appropriate:

00	Category of material
01	Specific material designation

Control field: 008

Code at least the following positions:

06	Type of date/Publication status
07-10	Date 1
11-14	Date 2
15-17	Place of publication, production or execution
22	Target audience
23	Form of item
28	Government publication
33	Literary form

34   Biography
35-37 Language
38   Modified record code
39   Cataloging source

010 field: Library of Congress control number (LCCN)

Mandatory if applicable.

020 field: International standard book number (ISBN)

Mandatory if applicable.

040 field: Cataloging source

Bibliographic records for books that reflect the DCRM(B) core-level standard must contain the designation "dcrmb" in subfield ‡e of field 040.

042 field: Authentication code

For DCRM(B) core-level records contributed by members of the PCC BIBCO program, include the designation "pcc" in field 042. For other DCRM(B) core records, leave the field blank.

050, 082, 086, 090, etc., fields: Call numbers

Assignment of at least one classification number from an established classification system recognized in *MARC 21 Format for Bibliographic Data* is encouraged, but not mandatory.

Since institutional practices for rare books often involve locally formulated call numbers, a requirement for a national standard classification could cause additional or undue effort for creators of DCRM(B) core-level records. However, if an institution supplies standard call numbers to materials covered by the DCRM(B) core record standard, it is encouraged to add these numbers in the appropriate call number field.

1XX field: Main entry

Mandatory if applicable. Headings on all DCRM(B) core-level records contributed to BIBCO must also be supported by national-level authority records. Authority records are not required for headings on other DCRM(B) core-level records.

240 field: Uniform title

Mandatory if applicable. Supply a uniform title if it is known or can be readily inferred from the publication .

245-4XX fields

Mandatory if applicable. One of the basic differences between AACR2 and DCRM(B) is the method and extent to which bibliographic details (fields 245-4XX) are recorded. As to method, bibliographic details should be recorded as correctly as possible, according to the descriptive conventions expected for the field. As to extent, DCRM(B) provides some options for abridging descriptive fields, and creators of core-level records for rare books are encouraged to implement these options wherever appropriate.

245 field: Title statement

Subfield ‡a is mandatory; all other subfields are mandatory if applicable. Subfield ‡h is mandatory for microforms.

246 field: Varying form of title

Mandatory if applicable. Use judgment in assessing each item or collection and assign a complement of title variants that covers variations deemed important. The variants assigned are intended to reflect cataloger judgment and/or local institutional policy.

250 field: Edition statement

Mandatory if applicable.

260 field: Publication, distribution, etc. (Imprint)

Subfield ‡c is mandatory. Supply the data appropriate to subfields ‡a and ‡b if readily available; otherwise, use "[S.l.]" and "[s.n.]" as appropriate. All other subfields are mandatory if applicable.

300 field: Physical description

Subfield ‡a and subfield ‡c are mandatory. All other subfields are mandatory if applicable.

4XX fields: Series statements

Mandatory if applicable. Transcribe all series as found in the publication in either a 490 or a 440 field. For DCRM(B) core-level records being contributed to BIBCO, all traced series must be supported by a national-level authority record. Untraced series need not be supported by a national-level authority record. If a national-level series authority record already exists for the series, follow the first tracing practice indicated on the record and record the series and tracing appropriately (i.e., in a 490 field, a 440 field or a 490/8XX pairing).

5XX fields: Notes

In DCRM(B) core-level records, a note indicating the transposition of any title area elements in the transcription is mandatory if applicable. Other notes are not required in DCRM(B) core, except as indicated below, although they may be included, if considered important. Notes are not required to justify added entries.

500 field: Source of title proper (if other than chief source)

Mandatory if applicable.

501 field: With note

Mandatory if applicable.

502 field: Dissertation note

Mandatory if applicable.

505 field: Formatted contents note

Mandatory if applicable. Supply as appropriate for collections, compilations, or for multipart monographs with separate titles.

510 field: Citation/references note

Addition of citation notes as a means of abbreviating detailed description of the publication is encouraged. Prefer sources that provide the fullest or most authoritative information, to keep the number of citations to a minimum.

6XX fields: Subject headings

Mandatory if applicable. Use judgment in assessing the publication and, if appropriate, assign a complement of headings that provides access to the primary/essential subject of the work (as opposed to secondary or tertiary aspects) at the appropriate level of specificity. Assign such headings from an established thesaurus or subject heading system recognized by the *MARC 21 Format for Bibliographic Data*. In focusing on the primary subject, follow the conventions of the particular subject heading system being used, including the use of paired or related headings where necessary to represent the subject fully.

655 field: Genre/form headings

Addition of genre/form terms to the DCRM(B) core-level record is encouraged if local policy calls for use of such terms, as appropriate to the piece. Prefer terms found in the official thesauri maintained by the RBMS Bibliographic Standards Committee;[25] terms from other authorized thesauri (e.g., the *Art and Architecture Thesaurus*) may also be used as appropriate.

7XX fields: Added entries

Mandatory if applicable. Use judgment in assessing each item and assign a complement of added entries that covers the primary relationships associated with the manifestation of which the item is a part. The inclusion and importance of added entries are intended to reflect individual cataloger's judgment and/or local institutional policy.

Headings on all DCRM(B) core-level records contributed to BIBCO must be supported by national-level authority records. Authority records are not required for headings on other DCRM(B) core-level records.

8XX fields: Series added entries

Mandatory if applicable.

---

[25] These thesauri include: *Binding Terms*; *Genre Terms*; *Paper Terms*; *Printing and Publishing Evidence*; *Provenance Evidence*; and *Type Evidence*.

APPENDIX D. MINIMAL-LEVEL RECORDS

D1. Introduction

The elements of description provided in DCRM(B) constitute a full set of information for describing rare materials. This appendix sets out a less than full level of description containing those elements recommended as a minimum for effective description of early printed books and other rare materials.

Libraries most often turn to minimal-level cataloging for rare materials in response to a need to create item-level records for large backlogs of uncataloged materials with the least amount of time and effort possible. These guidelines are provided in response to such needs. Their purpose is not to promote the use of DCRM(B) minimal-level cataloging, but rather to provide a usable standard for those institutions wishing to adopt it.

D2. Application

Catalogers may apply the minimal-level standard to any rare materials described using DCRM(B). DCRM(B) minimal-level records are especially appropriate when faithful and accurate descriptions are desirable, the provision of subject and other access points is not necessarily important, and abridged transcriptions and fewer notes are acceptable.

A minimal-level cataloging policy is best kept simple. Complex rules for omitting or shortening a variety of record elements would require catalogers to devote time to learning these new rules, thereby eliminating a portion of the intended gains in time and expense. In addition, tampering with the full description provided by DCRM(B) areas 0-6 and 8 would negate the very purpose of using DCRM(B) for description of rare materials. The conclusion then is that eliminating notes accomplishes much of the purpose of minimal-level cataloging because it saves considerable time while not unduly limiting access. Bibliographic records following this approach will, in most cases, still identify the books being described and distinguish them from similar editions or issues.

D3. Elements of the bibliographic record

D3.1. Follow the rules in DCRM(B) areas 0-6 and 8. Abridge the description wherever possible as allowed by the rules. It is not necessary to make the notes usually considered required.

D3.2. *Optionally*, add any additional elements in accordance with institutional policy. In particular, consider adding one or more of the following, each of which can significantly enhance the value of minimal-level DCRM(B) records for identifying rare materials:

- references to published descriptions in standard bibliographies (rule 7B14), particularly when the source cited provides more detailed information than the minimal-level bibliographic record

- the required notes called for in DCRM(B) (rules 2C2, 4A2.2, etc.)

- one or more local notes describing provenance, copy numbering, imperfections, binding, or any other information that will allow the bibliographic record to describe the particular copy in hand with sufficient precision to indicate the institution's ownership of that particular copy

- optional notes based on reliable dealers' descriptions accompanying the item being described

D3.3. Minimal-level cataloging policies often eliminate or simplify additional areas of the bibliographic record such as subject headings, classification, or other access points. This appendix does not address such questions, but users of DCRM(B) may also wish to streamline these areas according to local needs, taking into consideration the effect that such policies will have on special files for printers, binders, bindings, genre/forms, provenance, and the like.

Appendix E. Variations Requiring a New Record

E1. Default guidelines

E1.1. This appendix addresses the issue of whether to describe bibliographic variants using a single bibliographic record or separate records. As a default approach, the rules contained in DCRM(B) assume that a separate bibliographic record will be created for each bibliographic variant that represents what is referred to as an "edition" in AACR2 and an "issue" in bibliographic scholarship.

E1.2. Following this default approach, generally consider that a new bibliographic record is required whenever the publication distinguishes itself from other variants by one or more of the following characteristics:

- change in content (e.g., changes in the title, statement of responsibility, or edition statement that indicate corrections, revisions, expansions, abridgments, or the inclusion of supplementary materials)

- different setting of type (e.g., changes in the statement of extent, a change in bibliographic format, or differences in line-endings and catchwords revealed by the comparison of multiple copies)

- change in publication status (e.g., an original title page has been cancelled and replaced; an original publication, distribution, etc., statement has been covered with a new label; original sheets have been issued in a new publisher's cover bearing more recent data than that provided on the title page, or with a new series title page)

E1.3. In general, do not consider differences relating solely to substantially unchanged impressions, states, binding variants, or copies as an indication that a new record is required. Examples of differences that do not *in themselves* necessarily signal the need for a new record in the absence of other differences include:

- a difference in a statement of printing (e.g., fifth printing)

- a difference in the printer or other manufacturer if the publisher has not changed

- a difference in the printing or copyright date if the publication date has not changed

- a difference in the publisher's cover that does not provide evidence of a discrete publishing unit (e.g., a change of color in publisher's cloth)

‣ a difference relating to inserted publisher's advertisements and catalogs (unless they are integral to the publication)

‣ stop-press corrections

‣ the presence or absence of an errata slip

‣ the addition, deletion, or change of an ISBN

E1.4. These basic default guidelines result in a single bibliographic record being used to represent multiple impressions, states, and binding variants relating to a single edition or issue. This record may include, in local notes, information that does not apply to all copies of the edition or issue, whether the information applies to an impression, a state, a binding variant or an individual item.

E2. Alternative guidelines

E2.1. The default approach presented above is not prescriptive and indeed may not be desirable in every situation. Institutions may sometimes want to create separate records for different impressions or for other bibliographic variants. Some may want to create separate records for each individual copy.

E2.2. Numerous factors will influence the decision of when to create separate bibliographic records for variants, including:

‣ the comprehensiveness of an institution's collections

‣ the perceived needs of the users of these collections

‣ whether and how the publication has been described in a standard bibliography

‣ whether the publication can be compared to other copies

‣ the desire for consistency with other records in the institution's catalog

‣ the quality of the records available for use in copy cataloging

‣ the structure of any shared database to which an institution contributes its records

‣ the nature of an institution's policies, priorities, and staffing levels

E2.3. Within the rules, alternatives are provided that allow a cataloger to create separate records for individual impressions, states, binding variants, or copies (see rules 2B3.2, 2B4.2, 2D2, 4G). The cataloger must be consistent in applying these alternative rules to all areas of the description once the decision has been made to apply them.

Appendix F. Title Access Points

F1. Introduction

Title access plays an important role in enabling users to identify and locate special collections materials. While some title access will be handled by controlled forms, this appendix lists specific situations, commonly encountered by rare materials catalogers, in which the provision of uncontrolled title access points is likely to be useful.

The appendix is not intended as an exhaustive list of all instances in which uncontrolled title access points may be made. Use judgment in determining which forms of access will be most useful for the item in hand. In general, do not include access points that duplicate normalized forms of existing title access points (e.g., the title proper, a uniform title, etc.). Take the indexing capabilities of the institution's local system into consideration when determining whether the additional access points are needed.

F2. Rules relevant to the provision of title access points

The list is presented in DCRM(B) rule number order. Title access points considered optional are labeled as such.

0B1. Title proper

Provide access for the entire title proper exactly as transcribed, disregarding initial articles as required by filing rules.

0F1.1. Title proper in nonroman script

If nonroman text has been transcribed within the first five words of the title proper, provide additional title access for a romanized version of the title proper using the *ALA-LC Romanization Tables*.

> *Transcription*:
> 平家 物語
>
> *Additional title access*:
> Heike monogatari

0G2.2. Title proper with converted letters i/j or u/v

If any of the first five words in the title proper contains a letter **i/j/u/v** that has been converted to uppercase or lowercase according to a pattern of usage that follows pre-modern spelling conventions, provide additional title access for the form of the title proper that corresponds to modern orthography (i.e., using **i** and **u** for vowels, **j** and **v** for consonants, and **w** for consonantal **vv**).

If it differs from title access points already provided, also provide title access for the form of the title proper that corresponds to the graphical appearance of the letters in the source, converting the letters **i/j/u/v** into uppercase or lowercase without regard for the pattern of usage in the publication being described.

> *Source*:
> LES OEVVRES MORALES DE PLVTARQVE
>
> *Transcription*:
> Les oeuures morales de Plutarque
>
> *Additional title access (normalized modern)*:
> Oeuvres morales de Plutarque
>
> *Additional title access (converted graphical)*:
> Oevvres morales de Plvtarqve

0G2.3. Latin title proper with final capital I representing ii

If any of the first five words in the title proper is a Latin word with a final capital **I** that has been retained in the transcription, provide additional title access for the form of title proper with the final capital **I** converted to **ii**.

> *Source*:
> M. AccI Plauti quae supersunt Comoediae
>
> *Transcription*:
> M. AccI Plauti quae supersunt Comoediae
>
> *Additional title access*:
> M. Accii Plauti quae supersunt Comoediae

0G3.7. Title proper containing characters as substitutes for letters (Optional)

If a title proper contains hyphens or other characters as substitutes for letters, and the meaning of the characters is known, provide additional access to the decoded form of the title.

0G4.2. Title proper with inserted spacing

If any spacing has been inserted in the transcription of the first five words of the title proper, provide additional title access for the form of title with the words closed up.

> *Source*:
> LAMORTE D'ORFEO
>
> *Transcription*:
> La morte d'Orfeo
>
> *Additional title access*:
> Lamorte d'Orfeo

0G6.4. Title proper with an interpolated blank

If a blank space intended to be filled in manuscript has been transcribed within the first five words of the title proper as the word "blank" enclosed in square brackets, provide additional title access for the form of title proper without the interpolated blank.

> *Transcription*:
> This certifies that [blank] by a contribution of [blank] is a
>   member for life of the American Tract Society
>
> *Additional title access*:
> This certifies that by a contribution of is a member for life of
>   the American Tract Society

0G7.1. Title proper with corrected misprint

If any of the first five words in the title proper contains a misprint that has been corrected in the transcription through the insertion of **[i.e. ...]**, provide additional title access for the form of title proper as it appears in the source, without the correction. In addition, provide title access for the form of title as if it had been printed correctly.

Source:
The notted history of Mother Grim

Transcription:
```
The notted [i.e. noted] history of Mother Grim
```

Additional title access (without interpolation):
```
Notted history of Mother Grim
```

Additional title access (with correct spelling):
```
Noted history of Mother Grim
```

If any of the first five words in the title proper contains a misprint that has been qualified in the transcription by the insertion of **[sic]**, provide additional title access for the form of title proper without the **[sic]**. In addition, provide title access for the form of title as if it had been printed correctly.

Source:
Of the knowledg whiche maketh a wise man

Transcription:
```
Of the knowledg [sic] whiche maketh a wise man
```

Additional title access (without interpolation):
```
Of the knowledg whiche maketh a wise man
```

Additional title access (with correct spelling):
```
Of the knowledge whiche maketh a wise man
```

0G7.1. Title proper with non-standard orthography (Optional)

If the title proper contains words spelled according to older or non-standard orthographic conventions, provide additional title access for the title spelled according to modern orthography.

0G7.2. Title proper with approximated letters

If any of the first five words in the title proper contains two letters used to approximate a third letter, provide additional title access for the form of title proper with the letters transcribed as set.

Source:
Die rveysse der Messz vnnd Geniessung des hochwirdigē Sacraments

> ```
> Die Weysse der Messz vnnd Geniessung des hochwirdige[n]
>    Sacraments
> ```
>
> *Additional title access*:
> ```
> Rveysse der Messz vnnd Geniessung des hochwirdigen Sacraments
> ```

0G8.2. Title proper with special marks of contraction (Optional)

If the title proper contains a cataloger's expansions of special marks of contraction, provide additional title access for the title as it appears in the publication, ignoring the marks of contraction. In addition, provide title access for the transcribed form of the title proper, but without the square brackets.

> *Transcription*:
> ```
> Sermones Bertra[n]di de tempore et de sanctis
> ```
>
> *Additional title access (without expansion)*:
> ```
> Sermones Bertradi de tempore et de sanctis
> ```
>
> *Additional title access (without square brackets)*:
> ```
> Sermones Bertrandi de tempore et de sanctis
> ```

0G10. Title proper with initials, etc. (Optional)

If the title proper contains initials, initialisms, or acronyms with internal spaces, provide additional title access for the title with the spaces closed up. Conversely, if the title proper contains initials, initialisms, or acronyms without internal spaces, provide title access for the title with the spaces inserted.

1B1.1. Title proper with transposed elements (Optional)

If an element appearing before the title proper on the title page has been transposed, provide additional title access for the title inclusive of the preceding element. If the preceding element has not been transposed, so that the title proper includes it, provide additional title access for the title without the preceding element.

1B3.2. Title proper inclusive of an alternative title (Optional)

Provide additional title access for an alternative title.

1B6. Title proper with supplementary or section title (Optional)

Provide additional title access for a title that is supplementary to, or a section of, another work when both titles, whether or not grammatically separable, are recorded together as the title proper. If the supplement or section title is a title such as "Supplement" or "Chapter one," however, and so is indistinctive and dependent for its meaning on the main title, generally do not provide additional access.

1C. Parallel titles (Optional)

Provide additional title access for a parallel title.

1E14. Phrases about notes, appendixes, etc. (Optional)

Provide additional title access for phrases concerning notes, appendixes, etc., if the phrase is distinctive and the additional access seems useful.

1F1-1F2. Titles of additional works (Optional)

For other than supplementary matter, provide access for the titles of additional works named on a title page without a collective title. Also, selectively provide access for titles of additional works found in such a publication although not named on the title page.

1G1-1G8. Titles of works on single-sheet publications (Optional)

Provide additional access for titles of individual works on a single-sheet publication, whether or not the publication has a collective title. Also provide access for at least the first five words in the first line of printing if they have not been transcribed as part of the title proper.

6B1. Title proper of series (Optional)

Provide access for the series title proper exactly as it appears in the publication, unless title access is provided using a uniform series title.

7B4-7B5. Title variants and other titles (Optional)

Provide additional access for cover titles, added title page titles, caption titles, half titles, running titles, spine titles, and significant other title information.

7B11. Titles of accompanying material (Optional)

Provide additional access for any separate title on accompanying material deemed useful.

7B19. Copy-specific titles (Optional)

Provide additional access for copy-specific titles, such as a binder's title.

Appendix G. Early Letter Forms and Symbols

G1. Introduction

This appendix provides guidance for transcription of archaic letter and character forms, including marks of punctuation, and archaic conventions of contraction. Although this appendix cannot be exhaustive, it is intended to provide sufficient guidance for the most common occurrences, and to give a basis for judgment in ambiguous situations. For transcription of characters commonly found in signature statements that cannot be reproduced using available typographical facilities, see 7B9.2.

G2. Early letter forms and symbols

According to the instructions for transcription in rule 0G1.1, earlier forms of letters and symbols are converted to their modern forms.

Early letter forms and symbols				
Source	*Transcription*	*Example*	*Transcription of example*	*Notes*
ꝺ	d	**ꝺethe**	dethe	
ꝝ ÿ	ij	**alijs** **ooghelijck**	alijs ooghelijck	Ligatured italic **ij** may look like **ÿ**
k	k			Typical in early French signatures
cIꝺ Iꝺ	M D	**cIꝺIꝺCC v**	MDCCV	Inverted **C** used to form Roman numeral **M** or **D** is called an apostrophus
ꝛ ꝛ	r	**foꝛ**	for	
ſ ſ ſ	s	**refuſe**	refuse	Long **s** (an **f** has a crossbar on the stem; the bar on a long **s**, if present, extends from one side only)

ꝼ ß ſ ß	ss	deſß	dess	
ß	sz	Deſß	desz	Long s and **z** are spaced normally, no ligature
ꝛ	-	Weſt=Riding	West-Riding	
°	o	můß	mŭss	
ͤ	..	bů̈che	Büche	Superscript **e** functioning as an umlaut
& & ⁊ Ꜩ	&	ꝛc.	&c.	

G3. Early contractions

According to the instructions for transcription in rule 0G8.2, symbols of contraction used in continuance of the manuscript tradition are expanded to their full form, with cataloger-supplied letters or words enclosed in square brackets. The values of many contractions are dependent on context, with the most common values provided here.

Early contractions				
Source	*Transcription*	*Example*	*Transcription of example*	*Notes*
◌̄	[missing letter(s)]	cōſummatū dn̄s	co[n]summatu[m] D[omi]n[u]s	Over a vowel, usually **n** or **m**; over a consonant, often replaces several letters
ę	[ae]	hęc	h[ae]c	
xp̄s	[Christus]			A contraction using both Greek and Latin letters
ꝯ	[con]	ꝯcoꝛᵈ	[con]cor[di]a	

₃ ₃	[es] [ius] [us]	ſtatutꝫ roſſꝫ cuꝫ eiꝫ	statut[es] Ross[es] cu[ius] ei[us]	A highly versatile symbol; see also, for example, "[habet]," "[que]," "[scilicet]" and "[sed]" below
bꝫ	[habet]			
ħ	[hoc]			
ꝑ	[per] [par]	ſuꝑ ꝑticulari⁹	su[per] [par]ticulari[bus]	
ꝓ	[pro]	ꝓpter	[pro]pter	
ṗ	[pri]	ṗma	[pri]ma	
q̃	[quam]	vnq̃	vn[quam]	
q̃	[quan]	q̃tum	[quan]tum	
ꝙ q̃ q;	[que]	quoꝙ herculeæq; quoſq;	quo[que] Herculeae[que] quos[que]	
ꝗ	[qui]	ꝗb⁹	[qui]b[us]	
ꝙ	[quia]			
å	[quo]			
qꝋ qd'	[quod]			
r̃c.	[recta]			
ꝝ ꝶ	[rum]	quoꝝ libroꝝ	quo[rum] libro[rum]	
ſcꝫ	[scilicet]			
ſꝫ	[sed]			
y	[th]	ẙ ẙ	[the] [that]	When **y** is used to represent the Old English/Icelandic character **þ** [thorn], enclose **th** plus additional letters in square brackets.

z	[ur]	na∫cunt*z*	nascunt[ur]	
9	[us] [bus]	**reb9** **pticulari9**	reb[us] [par]ticulari[bus]	Superscript; a similar character at baseline represents "[con]"
ꝟ	[ver]	**ꝟtuo∫o**	[ver]tuoso	

G4. Letters i/j and u/v

G4.1. Historical background. Some knowledge of the history of printing as it applies to the letters **i/j** and **u/v** is helpful when applying the provisions of 0G2.2.

Until the early seventeenth century, the standard Latin alphabet contained 23 letters. The letters we know as **i** and **j** were considered different minuscule shapes (or graphs) of the same letter, as were the letters **u** and **v**. The letter **w** was not part of the standard Latin alphabet. A printer's choice for the **u** graph in preference to the **v** graph (or the **i** to the **j**) depended on its placement in a word and was governed by convention. Conventions varied somewhat from printer to printer, but often reflected national and regional preferences. While there were variant graphs for lowercase letters, in the pre-modern distribution there was only one graph for each of these letters used as capitals: **I** (with the gothic form resembling a modern **J**), and **V** (with the gothic form resembling a modern **U**). For example, **𝕵acob** = Iacob; **𝖀n∫potted** = Vnspotted (capitalized as the first word of a title).

The dominant patterns in use before the seventeenth century were:

› **i** used in the initial, medial, and final position, without signifying vocalic or consonantal use; e.g., iustice (modern form: justice)

› **j** used in the medial or final position only after a preceding **i** (more typical on the European continent), signifying vocalic use; e.g., commentarij (modern form: commentarii)

› **u** used in the initial, medial or final position, without signifying vocalic or consonantal use; e.g., oeuures (modern form: oeuvres)

› **v** used in the initial position, without signifying vocalic or consonantal use; e.g., vtilita (modern form: utilita)

› **I** used in all positions, without signifying vocalic or consonantal use; e.g., Iuan (modern form: Juan)

› **V** used in all positions, without signifying vocalic or consonantal use; e.g., Vrsprung (modern form: Ursprung)

A gradual shift took place over time, from the late fifteenth century through the middle of the seventeenth century, with **U/u** coming to phonetically signify a vowel and **V/v** to signify a consonant, regardless of case or position in the word. Likewise with **i** and **j**, although that shift was more irregular, with **I/i** coming to phonetically signify a vowel and **J/j** a consonant. In the modern 26-letter Latin alphabet, **i** and **j** and **u** and **v** are all considered separate letters.

G4.2. Transcription. As instructed in rule 0G2.2, when the rules for capitalization require converting **i/j** or **u/v** to uppercase or lowercase,[26] the cataloger is to follow the pattern of usage in the publication being described. Establish the pattern of usage by examining text in the same typeface (i.e., roman, italic, or gothic) in the publication being described. Identify examples of **i**, **j**, **u**, and **v** having the same function (vowel or consonant) and same relative position (appearing in initial, medial, or final positions) as the letters to be converted. Begin by examining the remainder of the title page and then, if necessary, proceed to examine the body of the text in other parts of the book in the same typeface. If the pattern of usage cannot be determined within a reasonable amount of time, use this conversion table as a solution of last resort.

Uppercase letter to be converted	*Lowercase conversion*
I (vowel or consonant) anywhere in word[27]	i
II at end of word	ij
II elsewhere in word	ii
V (vowel or consonant) at beginning of word	v
V (vowel or consonant) elsewhere in word	u
VV representing single letter[28]	vv

---

[26] An uppercase **J** or **U** in the source signals a modern distribution, in which **i** and **j** are functioning as separate letters, as are **u** and **v**, requiring no special consideration while converting case.

[27] Do not convert a final uppercase **I** meant to represent an **ii** ending (see 0G2.3).

Lowercase letter to be converted	Uppercase conversion
i (vowel or consonant) anywhere in word	I
j (vowel or consonant) anywhere in word	I
u (vowel or consonant) anywhere in word	V
v (vowel or consonant) anywhere in word	V
vv representing single letter[28]	VV

G5. Letter w

G5.1. Historical background. The representation of the letter **w** is not to be confused with the developments of the **u/v** graphs. The **w** graph was part of the standard alphabet for Germanic languages. Most early printing was in Latin, shifting gradually to include a greater proportion of vernacular languages throughout Europe. **W** and **w** must have been scanty in cases of Roman type, and they appear to have been frequently exhausted when setting text in Dutch, English, or German. When that happened, compositors usually did one of two things: used **VV** or **vv** to stand in for **W** or **w**, or permanently altered **V** or **v** type pieces—achieved by filing or shaving one of the serifs, often the right serif on the left piece—so that the two type pieces would sit closely together in the forme, thereby more closely resembling a **w**. In early German texts, printers sometimes used a curved **r** followed by a **v** to approximate a **w**.

G5.2. Transcription. When **VV** and **vv** graphs have been used to represent the single letter **W** or **w**, transcribe them as **VV** or **vv** as appropriate. When there is clear evidence of the filing of one or both pieces of type showing the intention of creating the **W** or **w** graph, transcribe as **W** or **w**, making an explanatory note, if considered important. In cases of doubt, transcribe as **VV** and **vv**. When separate **rv** graphs have been used by the printer to approximate the single letter **W** or **w**, transcribe as **W** or **w**, making an explanatory note, if considered important (see 0G7.2).

---

[28] This must be distinguished from **VV** or **vv** as a combination of a vowel and a consonant as in the examples VVLT or vvlt (vult, "he wants") and VVA or vva (uva, "grape").

Forms of W				
Source	*Transcription*	*Example*	*Transcription of example*	*Notes*
VV	vv	VVhole	vvhole	
W	w	WHOLE	whole	
⁊v	w	⁊veyße	weysse	

Appendix H. Individual and Special Issues of Serials

Apply these guidelines when creating a bibliographic record for an individual or special issue of a serial, whether or not also creating a record for the serial as a whole. Individual and special issues may be cataloged as monographs and related to the serial as a whole.

H1. Bibliographic level

The bibliographic level for an issue of a serial is **m** (monograph), just as it is for an individual part of a multipart monograph cataloged separately.

H2. Body of the description

H2.1. General rule

Formulate the body of the description according to the rules in DCRM(B). Transcribe information in the form and order in which it is presented in the source, unless instructed otherwise by specific rules (see 0G).

H2.2. Issues with distinctive titles

If the issue has a distinctive title, transcribe that title in the title and statement of responsibility area.

H2.3. Issues without distinctive titles

H2.3.1. If the issue has no distinctive title, transcribe the title of the serial and the numbering of the issue (including numeric and/or chronological designations) in the title and statement of responsibility area.

```
245  04  ‡a The post boy. ‡n Numb. 2436, from Thursday December
             21 to Saturday December 23, 1710.

245  04  ‡a The American printer. ‡p Franklin bi-centennial
             number. ‡n January 20, 1923.

245  14  ‡a The foundling hospital for wit : ‡b intended for the
             reception and preservation of such brats of wit and
             humour whose parents chuse to drop them. ‡n Number
             III, to be continued occasionally / ‡c by Timothy
             Silence, Esq.
```

H2.3.2. If the issue numbering appears at the head of title, transpose it and make a note indicating the transposition (see 1B6).

H2.3.3. If the issue numbering appears following a statement of responsibility, transcribe it as a subsequent statement of responsibility.

H3. Relating individual issues to the serial as a whole

H3.1. General rule

To relate the description of an individual issue to the description of the serial as a whole and to provide organized access to the records in the catalog, make a series added entry using the uniform title for the serial. Apply AACR2 and LCRI in formulating the uniform title.

H3.2. Issues with distinctive titles

For access to the serial title on a monographic record for an issue that has a distinctive title, give a simple series statement (440) if the serial title will be traced in the form in which it appears on the piece. If the serial title appearing on the piece is not in the form in which it will be traced, give an uncontrolled series statement (490) with a series added entry (8XX).

```
245  02   ‡a A book of humorous limericks / ‡c edited by Clement
              Wood.
440   0   ‡a Little blue book ; ‡v no. 1018

245  00   ‡a Earthquake potential in Colorado.
490   1   ‡a Bulletin / Colorado Geological Survey, Department of
              Natural Resources, State of Colorado ; ‡v 43
830   0   ‡a Bulletin (Colorado Geological Survey) ; ‡v 43.
```

H3.3. Issues without distinctive titles

For access to the serial title on a monographic record for an issue that does not have a distinctive title, give a series added entry (8XX).

```
245  14   ‡a The foundling hospital for wit : ‡b intended for the
              reception and preservation of such brats of wit and
              humour whose parents chuse to drop them. ‡n Number
              III, to be continued occasionally / ‡c by Timothy
              Silence, Esq.
800   1   ‡a Silence, Timothy. ‡t Foundling hospital for wit ; ‡v
              no. 3.
```

```
245  00  ‡a Hoopoe. ‡n Spring 1991, issue no. 7.
830   0  ‡a Hoopoe ; ‡v issue no. 7.

245  00  ‡a Almanacco anti letterario Bompiani. ‡n 1937-XV.
830   0  ‡a Almanacco anti letterario Bompiani ; ‡v 1937.
```

H3.4. Issue numbering

H3.4.1. General rule. Transcribe issue numbering (including numeric and/or chronological designations) in full in the descriptive areas, but standardize issue numbering in the added entry for the serial. This will provide both the accurate representation of individual issues as well as an organized display of sequential issues within the catalog.

```
245  04  ‡a The post boy ‡n Numb. 2436, from Thursday December 21
             to Saturday December 23, 1710.
830   0  ‡a Post boy (London, England) ; ‡v no. 2436.
```

H3.4.2. Chronological designation only. If the issue has only a chronological designation, use "year month day" as the standardized form of the chronological designation in the access point.

```
245  04  ‡a The English Lucian, or, Weekly discoveries of the
             witty intrigues, comical passages, and remarkable
             transactions in town and country with reflections on
             the vices and vanities of the times. ‡n Friday the
             17th of January, 1698.
830   0  ‡a English Lucian ; ‡v 1698 Jan. 17.
```

H4. Relating special issues to the serial as a whole

H4.1. Special issues

A special issue of a serial usually covers a particular topic. It may have a distinctive title or it may simply be called "special issue" or the equivalent. Some special issues are published within the numbering system of a serial; others are published outside the numbering system of a serial. The statement identifying a special issue as such may be presented formally in the publication or it may presented informally (e.g., embedded in text).

H4.2. Special issues outside the numbering of a serial

If the special issue is outside the numbering of the serial, relate the monograph to the serial title by giving a uniform title added entry (7XX) for the serial. If the statement identifying the special issue as such is not presented formally, give the information in a note in order to justify the added entry.

```
245   00   ‡a Champions in the sun : ‡b a special issue of
           California history, the magazine of the California
           Historical Society / ‡c Frances Ring, guest editor.
730    0   ‡a California history.

245   04   ‡a The trout season of 1883 : ‡b the trout of American
           waters.
500        ‡a "The American angler. A weekly journal of fish and
           fishing. Special issue for the trout season of
           1883"--P. [1].
730    0   ‡a American angler (New York, N.Y. : 1881)
```

H4.3. Special issues within the numbering of a serial

Special issues that are published within the numbering of the serial are related to the serial by means of a simple series statement (440) if the serial title will be traced in the form in which it appears on the piece. If the serial title appearing on the piece is not in the form in which it will be traced, give an uncontrolled series statement (490) with a series added entry (8XX). If the statement identifying the special issue as such is not presented formally, give the information in a note in order to justify the added entry.

```
100    1   ‡a Berrigan, Ted.
245   10   ‡a Carrying a torch / ‡c Ted Berrigan.
500        ‡a "Published as Clown war 22 in January 1980"--P. [2]
           of cover.
830    0   ‡a Clown war ; ‡v 22.

245   00   ‡a Chelsea retrospective 1958-1983.
490    1   ‡a Chelsea, ‡x 0009-2185 ; ‡v 42/43
500        ‡a "25th anniversary, 1958/1982"--P. [4] of cover.
830    0   ‡a Chelsea (New York, N.Y.) ; ‡v 42/43.

245   04   ‡a The black press : ‡b special issue.
490    1   ‡a Harvard journal of Afro-American affairs ; ‡v volume
           2, number 2, 1971
830    0   ‡a Harvard journal of Afro-American affairs ; ‡v v. 2,
           no. 2.
```

H5. Relating separately published monographs to the serial as a whole

Serial issues with distinctive titles may also have been published separately as monographs. Do not treat these monographs as part of the serial. When cataloging such a monograph, make a note to indicate that the title was also published as an issue of the serial. Give a uniform title added entry (7XX) for the serial.

```
245  04   ‡a The forbidden stitch : ‡b an Asian American women's
              anthology / ‡c edited by Shirley Geok-lin Lim, Mayumi
              Tsutakawa, Margarita Donnelly (managing editor).
500        ‡a "Also published as vol. 11 #2&3 of Calyx, a journal
              of art and literature by women"--Half-title verso.
730  0    ‡a Calyx (Corvallis, Or.)

245  04   ‡a The black revolution : ‡b an Ebony special issue.
500        ‡a "First published as a special issue of Ebony magazine
              August, 1969"--T.p. verso.
730  0    ‡a Ebony (Chicago, Ill.)
```

H6. Linking records for individual issues to the serial record

Optionally, when cataloging an individual issue of a serial, provide a linking entry between the record for the individual issue and the record for the serial as a whole by means of a host item entry (773):

```
773  0    ‡a Silence, Timothy. ‡t Foundling hospital for wit. ‡g
              No. 3

773  0    ‡a Post boy (London, England). ‡g No. 2436
```

GLOSSARY

This glossary is intended to supplement the glossary in AACR2, Appendix D. The terms included here are either lacking in AACR2, or, though present there, require some amendment to accommodate these rules to the description of special printed materials. The definitions marked with an asterisk have been derived from G. Thomas Tanselle's "The bibliographical concepts of issue and state," in *The Papers of the Bibliographical Society of America*, 69 (1975), p. 17-66.

Bibliographic description. A set of bibliographic data recording and identifying a publication, i.e., the description that begins with the title proper and ends with the last note.

Broadside, broadsheet. *See* **Single-sheet publication**.

Cancellation. A substitution for something originally printed. Usually applies to leaves but may apply to portions of leaves, pairs of leaves, or entire gatherings. The replacement leaf, etc., is called the cancel or cancellans (plural cancels or cancellantia). The original leaf, etc., is variously called the cancelled leaf, the uncancelled leaf (if it is still present), the cancelland, or the cancellandum (plural cancellanda).

Chief title. The distinguishing word or sequence of words that names a publication, as given on the title page (or substitute). This definition excludes alternative titles, parallel titles, other title information, and subsidiary title information preceding the chief title on the title page, such exclusion resulting usually in a short title. *See also* **Title proper**.

Chronogram. A phrase, sentence, or other text in which the numeric values of certain letters (usually distinguished typographically) express a date when added together.

Device. A printed design, generally symbolic, emblematic, or pictorial rather than textual, used to identify a printer, bookseller, or publisher. To be distinguished from a logo that renders a name as a stylized, primarily textual design.

Docket title. A title written, typed, or printed on a document, or on a label affixed to the document, briefly indicating its contents or subject. Usually found perpendicular to the main text, on an otherwise blank page (e.g., the verso of the last leaf), on a document designed to be folded for filing.

*Edition. All copies resulting from a single job of typographical composition.

Fingerprint. A group of characters selected from specific locations in the publication, which, when combined with the date of publication, etc., serves to identify a book as having been printed from a certain setting of type.

Gathering. One or more pairs of leaves—made up of a folded sheet, a fraction of a sheet, or several folded sheets tucked one inside another—that together form a distinct unit for binding purposes. *See also* **Signature**.

Illustration. A pictorial, diagrammatic, or other graphic representation occurring within a publication, excepting minor decorative elements such as vignettes, head- and tail-pieces, historiated initials, and printers' ornaments.

Impression. All copies produced in the course of one printing event; the term is synonymous with "printing."

Integral. 1. A leaf is integral to a gathering if it is conjugate with another leaf in the gathering. 2. A leaf is integral to a publication if it can be assumed to be present in all copies represented by the bibliographic description. Leaves added after publication by an owner (e.g., extra-illustrated copies) or by a binder are not considered integral to the publication and thus must be described in local notes.

*Issue. A group of published copies which constitutes a consciously planned publishing unit, distinguishable from other groups of published copies by one or more differences designed expressly to identify the group as a discrete unit.

Leaf of plates. A plate in a publication that also has one or more leaves or pages of text (whether preliminary text or text proper). Plates may be described in terms of pages of plates if they are numbered as pages or are unnumbered and have illustrative matter on both sides. *See also* **Plate**.

Letterpress. Printing done directly from raised surfaces. Includes printing done from type, from wood blocks (e.g., woodcuts and wood-engravings), and from metal surfaces designed for relief printing (e.g., stereotypes and electrotypes).

Panel. A rectangular section formed by the creases in a single-sheet publication that has been issued folded but is intended to be used unfolded.

Perfect copy. A copy of a publication that is physically complete and correctly arranged, as issued.

Plate. A leaf that is chiefly or entirely non-letterpress, or a folded leaf of any kind, inserted with letterpress gatherings of text. A plate usually contains illustrative matter, with or without accompanying text, but may contain only text (e.g., an engraved title page or a folded letterpress table). *See also* **Leaf of plates.**

Signature. A letter, numeral, symbol, or a group of such characters, printed at the foot of the rectos of the first few leaves of an intended gathering for the purpose of aiding binders in correctly assembling the sections. *See also* **Gathering**.

Single-sheet publication. A publication printed on a single or composite piece of paper or other material; it may be printed on one or both sides and may be bound or unbound. The content of a single-sheet publication, as here defined, is predominantly textual in nature, though it may contain illustrations that are subordinate or coordinate to the text. (See 5B2 for normally imposed single sheets and 5B14 for single sheets designed to be read unfolded.)

*State. A copy or a group of copies of a printed sheet or a publisher's casing which differs from other copies (within the same impression or issue) of that sheet or casing in any respect which the publisher does not wish to call to the attention of the public as representing a discrete publishing effort.

Title proper. The chief title of a publication, together with any title information preceding the chief title and any alternative title. This definition excludes parallel titles and any other title information following the chief title. *See also* **Chief title**.

Variant. A copy showing any bibliographically significant difference from one or more other copies of the same edition. The term may refer to an impression, issue, or state.

LIST OF WORKS CITED

ALA-LC Romanization Tables: *Transliteration Schemes for Non-Roman Scripts*. 1997 ed. Washington, D.C.: Cataloging Distribution Service, Library of Congress, 1997 (and updates). http://lcweb.loc.gov/catdir/cpso/roman.html

Anglo-American Cataloguing Rules. Joint Steering Committee for Revision of AACR. 2nd ed., 2002 revision. Ottawa: Canadian Library Association; Chicago: American Library Association, 2002 (and updates).

Art & Architecture Thesaurus. 2nd ed. New York: Oxford University Press, 1994. http://www.getty.edu/research/conducting_research/vocabularies/aat/

BIBCO Core Record Standards. Washington, D.C.: Program for Cooperative Cataloging, Library of Congress. http://www.loc.gov/catdir/pcc/bibco/coreintro.html

Binding Terms: *A Thesaurus for Use in Rare Book and Special Collections Cataloguing*. Standards Committee, Rare Books and Manuscripts Section. Chicago: Association of College and Research Libraries, 1988 (and updates). http://www.rbms.info/committees/bibliographic_standards/controlledvocabularies/

Cappelli, Adriano. *Cronologia e Calendario Perpetuo*. Milano: Ulrico Hoepli, 1906. [6. ed.: *Cronologia, Cronografia e Calendario Perpetuo*. Milano: Ulrico Hoepli, 1988]

Cheney, C.R. *Handbook of Dates for Students of English History*. London: Offices of the Royal Historical Society, 1945. [New ed., revised by Michael Jones: Cambridge; New York: Cambridge University Press, 2004]

The Chicago Manual of Style. 15th ed. Chicago: Chicago University Press, 2003.

"Collection-Level Cataloging." *Cataloging Service Bulletin*, no. 78 (Fall 1997), p. 8-28. Washington, D.C.: Library of Congress, Collections Services.

Describing Archives: *A Content Standard*. Chicago: Society of American Archivists, 2004.

Fingerprints = Empreintes = Impronte. Paris: Institut de Recherche et d'Histoire des Textes, 1984. [Supplemented by: *Nouvelles des Empreintes = Fingerprint*

Newsletter, no. 1- (1981-). Paris: Institut de Recherche et d'Histoire des Textes].

Functional Requirements for Bibliographic Records. IFLA Study Group on the Functional Requirements for Bibliographic Records. München: K.G. Saur, 1998. http://www.ifla.org/VII/s13/frbr/frbr.htm

Gaskell, Philip. *A New Introduction to Bibliography*. Oxford: Oxford University Press, 1972. Corrections incorporated into subsequent reprintings. [1995 reprint: Winchester: St. Paul's Bibliographies; New Castle, Del.: Oak Knoll Press]

Genre Terms: *A Thesaurus for Use in Rare Book and Special Collections Cataloguing*. Bibliographic Standards Committee, Rare Books and Manuscripts Section. 2nd ed. Chicago: Association of College and Research Libraries, 1991 (and updates). http://www.rbms.info/committees/bibliographic_standards/controlledvocabularies/

ISBD(A): *International Standard Bibliographic Description for Older Monographic Publications (Antiquarian)*. 2nd rev. ed. München: K.G. Saur, 1991. http://www.ifla.org/VII/s13/pubs/isbda.htm

MARC 21 Format for Bibliographic Data. Network Development and MARC Standards Office, Library of Congress, in cooperation with Standards and Support, National Library of Canada. Washington, D.C.: Cataloging Distribution Service, Library of Congress, 1999 (and updates). Concise format: http://www.loc.gov/marc/bibliographic/ecbdhome.html

Merriam-Webster's Collegiate Dictionary. 11th ed. Springfield, Mass.: Merriam-Webster, 2003.

Paper Terms: *A Thesaurus for Use in Rare Book and Special Collections Cataloguing*. Bibliographic Standards Committee, Rare Books and Manuscripts Section. Chicago: Association of College and Research Libraries, 1990 (and updates). http://www.rbms.info/committees/bibliographic_standards/controlledvocabularies/

Printing and Publishing Evidence: *Thesauri for Use in Rare Book and Special Collections Cataloguing*. Standards Committee, Rare Books and Manuscripts Section. Chicago: Association of College and Research Libraries, 1986 (and updates). http://www.rbms.info/committees/bibliographic_standards/controlledvocabularies/

Provenance Evidence: *Thesaurus for Use in Rare Book and Special Collections Cataloguing.* Standards Committee, Rare Books and Manuscripts Section. Chicago: Association of College and Research Libraries, 1988 (and updates). http://www.rbms.info/committees/bibliographic_standards/controlledvocabularies/

"Relator Terms for Rare Book, Manuscript, and Special Collections Cataloguing." Standards Committee, Rare Books and Manuscripts Section, Association of College and Research Libraries. 3rd ed. *College & Research Libraries*, v. 48, no. 9 (Oct. 1987), p. 553-557. [Supplemented by correction note on p. 645, v. 48, no. 10 (Nov. 1987) and updates]. http://www.rbms.info/committees/bibliographic_standards/controlledvocabularies/

Roe, Kathleen. *Arranging and Describing Archives and Manuscripts.* Chicago: Society of American Archivists, 2005.

Svenonius, Elaine. *The Intellectual Foundation of Information Organization.* Cambridge: The MIT Press, 2000.

Tanselle, G. Thomas. "The Bibliographical Concepts of Issue and State." *Papers of the Bibliographical Society of America*, v. 69 (1975), p. 17-66.

Thesaurus for Graphic Materials. Washington, D.C.: Cataloging Distribution Service, Library of Congress, 1995. TGM II: http://www.loc.gov/rr/print/tgm2/

Type Evidence: *A Thesaurus for Use in Rare Book and Special Collections Cataloguing.* Bibliographic Standards Committee, Rare Books and Manuscripts Section. Chicago: Association of College and Research Libraries, 1990 (and updates). http://www.rbms.info/committees/bibliographic_standards/controlledvocabularies/

VanWingen, Peter M. and Belinda D. Urquiza. *Standard Citation Forms for Published Bibliographies and Catalogs Used in Rare Book Cataloging.* In collaboration with the Bibliographic Standards Committee, Rare Books and Manuscripts Section, Association of College and Research Libraries. 2nd ed. Washington, D.C.: Cataloging Distribution Service, Library of Congress, 1996.

Vriesema, P.C.A. "The STCN Fingerprint." *Studies in Bibliography*, v. 39 (1986), p. 93-100. http://etext.lib.virginia.edu/bsuva/sb/

INDEX

Symbols

A

C

D

E

H

I

O

P